PENNSYLVANIA COLLEGE OF TECHNOLOGY LIBR

5 0608 01 49 7

D1169083

Snapshots of Autism

of related interest

Asperger's Syndrome
A Guide for Parents and Professionals
Tony Attwood
Foreword by Lorna Wing
ISBN 1 85302 577 1

Freaks, Geeks and Asperger Syndrome
A User Guide to Adolescence
Luke Jackson
ISBN 1 84310 098 3

Living and Loving with Asperger Syndrome
The McCabe Family
ISBN 1 84310 744 9

Pretending to be Normal
Living with Asperger's Syndrome
Liane Holliday Willey
Foreword by Tony Attwood
ISBN 1 85302 749 9

Hitchhiking through Asperger Syndrome
Lise Pyles
Foreword by Tony Attwood
ISBN 1 85302 937 8

Snapshots of Autism

A Family Album

Jennifer Overton

Jessica Kingsley Publishers
London and New York

AUG 2 9 2003

LIBRARY

All rights reserved. No part of this publication may be reproduced in any
material form (including photocopying or storing it in any medium by
electronic means and whether or not transiently or incidentally to some other
use of this publication) without the written permission of the copyright owner
except in accordance with the provisions of the Copyright, Designs and Patents
Act 1988 or under the terms of a licence issued by the Copyright Licensing
Agency Ltd, 90 Tottenham Court Road, London, England W1P 9HE.
Applications for the copyright owner's written permission to reproduce any
part of this publication should be addressed to the publisher.

Warning: The doing of an unauthorised act in relation to a copyright work may
result in both a civil claim for damages and criminal prosecution.

The right of Jennifer Overton to be identified as author of this work has been
asserted by her in accordance with the Copyright, Designs and Patents Act
1988.

First published in the United Kingdom in 2003
by Jessica Kingsley Publishers Ltd
116 Pentonville Road
London N1 9JB, England
and
29 West 35th Street, 10th fl.
New York, NY 10001-2299, USA

www.jkp.com

Copyright © 2003 Jennifer Overton

Library of Congress Cataloging in Publication Data
A CIP catalog record for this book is available from the Library of Congress

British Library Cataloguing in Publication Data
A CIP catalogue record for this book is available from the British Library

ISBN 1 84310 723 6

Printed and Bound in Great Britain by
Athenaeum Press, Gateshead, Tyne and Wear

To Nicholas

My husband: my partner in life, art and autism.
Thank you for your inspiration, guidance, and patience.
In life, art, and autism.
I love you, David. Thank you for holding hands with
me on this journey.

Thanks also to Jessica,
for her encouragement and wisdom.

Contents

Dear Reader:

Between these covers are some written snapshots of our lives with our high-functioning autistic son, Nicholas.

A note about the structure of this 'scrapbook,' most family albums are well-organized, chronological, neat groupings of photos that you can leaf through and remember 'Oh, this was when Susie was five,' followed by a picture of Susie at six, with no front teeth, and then a picture of seven-year-old Susie in her second grade school play, and so on.

Not this collection of snapshots.

This book is more like a box of loose photos collected over a period of five years, dumped out onto the living room floor, sorted through and reflected upon.

The frame for these written snapshots is various special occasions throughout our calendar year. And, although these occasions are chronological and appear to span one year, the pieces themselves are drawn from different years.

As a result, the snapshots are random: a glimpse of our family at Christmas when Nicholas was five years old, perhaps followed by a glimpse of our family on New Year's Day when Nicholas was two, and so on.

Most important, this is a *family* album. And anyone who has been touched by autism, is, by the very nature of the experiences we share, part of this family.

It is my sincere hope that those of you who have, or know, or work with, or live with, or are otherwise blessed by someone with autism, will recognize the scenarios, the laughter, the joys, the challenges – will find yourselves pictured in this box of snapshots.

Jennifer Overton
January 2003

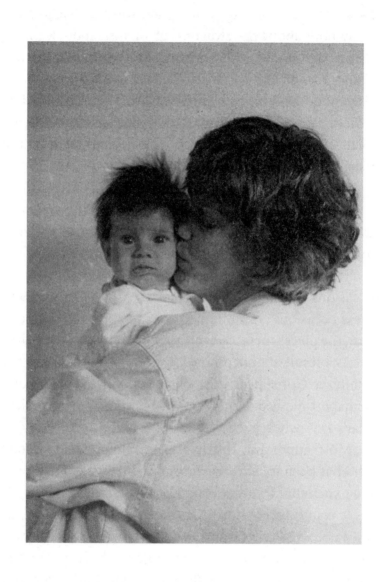

October 22nd: Nicholas' Birthday

A Letter to My Son

Last night I had a dream. I dreamed I was driving along a winding coastal road. All of a sudden a beautiful boy dressed in black and carrying a violin case crossed the road in front of me, causing me to stop. I asked him where he was going, and if I could give him a lift. He recited his address, an address I'd never heard, and got in the back seat. I looked in the rearview mirror and a wave of panic rose in me at the sight of his composed angelic face, staring straight ahead. In spite of my unease, I knew that I had to help him find his way home. I began driving. Searching. I woke up, my heart racing.

My son, My beautiful son,

Tomorrow is your fifth birthday. My big boy. My child. Five years old! Dad and I are so very proud of you. We are madly in love with you, and we wouldn't want you to be any different than you are. You are one terrific kid. Very special. And it was exactly one year ago today that you were diagnosed autistic.

Autistic. Autism. That word still kicks me right in the stomach. It knocks the wind out of me as much as it did the first time I heard it a year ago, in the cold blunt way we were told of your disorder. "Yup, it's autism, and it's never going to go away." I remember feeling like all my blood had left my body. And I remember hearing the cold

October rain slapping against the window of the white, sterile psychologist's office. It's one thing to harbour nagging suspicions; it's quite another to hear the word AUTISM from the mouth of a professional, and to see it in black and white. No longer deniable. Inescapable. Lifelong.

As much as we love you, it's been a very difficult year for me and Dad. Who can prepare for such a thing? It has been a year filled with tears, grief, numbness, panic, desperation, fear, love, determination, and anger. A lot of anger. Anger at a family doctor who repeatedly dismissed my concerns about your development; anger at a medical system that put us on fourteen-month-long waiting lists, and after diagnosing you, ushered us out the door with nothing more than a wave and a 'good luck'; anger that your neurological disorder is shrouded in mystery and stigma, and that the medical community offers no treatment.

I'm angry that I had to spend months reading, researching, desperately looking for information on how to help you with no one to guide me; I'm angry we don't live closer to my family; angry that there isn't something or someone to blame for this; I feel anger toward friends who have effortlessly developing children and still dare to complain; I'm angry at having been given this huge responsibility; angry because I can never rest; and yes, I'm angry at you for not giving me back things like hugs and kisses. My darling, it's very hard to keep giving when I don't get a lot back in return. Please try to understand. I know you can't help it, but that doesn't make it easier.

But mostly, I'm angry at myself. Angry and guilty for not having recognized the signs earlier, because early diagnosis and intervention have been proven to increase chances of full integration into society. I wish I hadn't hushed my concerns. I'm sorry. I'm so sorry. For not listening to myself. And for not listening to what you were telling me. And when you were diagnosed, I'm sorry for being sad. I want you to know that I am not sad about you, or that you are my son. Never. It's the world: I'm worried about you in this world.

Autism. It conjures images of a solitary, mute, rocking child. That's not you; it never was. But when I think back, and look at your baby book, I recognize what I now know to be the early signs. You screamed at the sound of tin foil being ripped. You stiffened when I held you. Your eye contact was not good. Instead of pushing toy cars around the living room, you turned them over and spun the wheels.

Numbers, letters, and shapes were your favourite play-things. At barely two years of age you pointed to a small eight-sided window and said, 'Octagon.' Before the age of three you were spelling words with blocks. I recall being in the car and hearing you mutter, 'Three, one, eighteen. That spells car.' It took me a while to figure out that what you had done was assign the letters of the alphabet numbers in your head, and were spelling words with the assigned numbers.

And your memory. Uncanny. Eerie. You sing songs after hearing them once. You remember where you dropped an elastic band three years ago. You remember the minutest detail, and forget nothing.

And yet you show little interest in playing with other children. Kids are loud; they move around a lot; they're unpredictable. Not only must it be an assault to your over-sensitive senses, but you don't know the rules to that game; the steps to that dance. You don't know how to make a friend. You don't know how to play.

Sometimes your literal mind offers up funny, poetic insights. "Mom, the scissors are clapping." "Mom, can you put your headache away?" Birds dance in the air, tummies cry when they're hungry, and anti-social is a relative coming to visit next week.

Dad and I celebrate your uniqueness. But will the world? Will the kids in school call you a computer with no feelings? A robot, to be turned on in the morning and off at night? Will you ever be invited to a sleepover? Will you learn to be a friend? Will you ever hug me and say, "I love you Mom." On good days I have faith that the world will be gentle. On bad days I just want to hold you in my arms and shelter you. My mysterious child in black, what is the road you're walking down? And where are you bound?

Tomorrow you turn five. We are so very proud of you. You are working hard to learn the life skills you are going to need. We love you. And we will do everything in our power to help you reach your full potential and be the happiest person you can be. And while we're busy teaching you the ways of this world, you can teach us a lesson or two about love, patience, commitment, and beauty. OK?

Happy Birthday son. And thanks for choosing our road to walk across.

Love, Mom

October 31st: Hallowe'en

Trick or Treat

"Do you want to come outside with me and set up the skeletons?" I ask, bending toward him and contorting my face into a scary grimace.

"No thank you, I prefer to play electronic Wheel of Fortune."

"OK. Do you want to bring it outside and sit on the rock while I decorate out there?"

"No."

I try to hide my disappointment at his reluctance to get into the spirit of the thing, and wonder who is the adult and who is the child in this household.

As far back as I can remember Hallowe'en has been one of my favourite days of the year. I'm not sure why. Maybe because October 31st allows us, for one day, to be childishly prankish and superstitious. Maybe it's because as a child, Hallowe'en gave license to my dramatic tendencies in an otherwise strictly religious household. Maybe because it justified my very real fear of ghosts, witches, and things under the bed that went bump in the night. Or maybe it's because now that I'm "all grown up," Hallowe'en is a refreshing and necessary time to revisit the dark and devilish side of my personality in the mature world of mortgage payments and retirement savings plans.

But more than that, I suspect I like Hallowe'en so much simply because it's 'scary.' A good Hallowe'en should perform the same spine-tingling duty as a good rollercoaster or scary movie. There is the possibility of danger at every turn: a walk into a tarantula's web, a big black furry beastie dropping onto you from above. The unexpected is to be expected. Superior reasoning gives itself over to animal instincts. Our nervous systems stand by on high alert: we wait in delicious anticipation of being frightened and startled out of our wits.

So it comes as no surprise that I take decorating for this occasion pretty seriously. No 'McHallowe'en.' No cutesy paper witches with wartless, smiling, kind faces hanging in our windows. No ma'am. And, as this is our first Hallowe'en in our new home, this year will offer exciting opportunities for creative spookosity: the graceful curved staircase the perfect place to weave spider-filled cobwebs; at the base a prime location for the placement of a couple of scowling-faced jack-o-lanterns; our tall front door ideal for rigging a threesome of life-size rubber bats rigged to swoop and dart over visitors' heads when the door is opened; and the stand of trees in the front yard presents vast possibilities for posing glow in the dark, three-dimensional skeletons, whether hanging by a noose from the highest branch of the tallest tree, or positioned on the ground as if seeming to crawl out of their graves.

Now, I'm not going to go so far as to say that I am so fanatical about Hallowe'en that we bought this house because of its Hallowe'en decorating potential, but just let me say that its suitability for this special occasion is one of its many charms.

So. I'm filled with anticipation.

My autistic son, on the other hand, is totally indifferent.

As I climb the stepladder and position the biggest skeleton among the highest branches of the tree at the end of the driveway, I smile as I remember past Hallowe'ens.

Nicholas was born in late October, and it was all my husband David could do to keep me from dressing the baby up that first Hallowe'en when he was just a week old, and taking him out trick or treating.

There was the year I dressed him up as a peanut butter sandwich. He was wrapped from head to toe in brown felt, and he had a piece of white posterboard in the shape of a slice of bread attached to his front and his back, from his shoulders to his shins. He looked hilarious. I felt brilliantly creative. He was oblivious to the fact that he was sporting a dynamic, highly original costume amidst the sea of Barneys and witches wandering the streets that night. Of course, he was only three at the time. And he hadn't been diagnosed yet.

And then there was the year he went out trick or treating dressed as the man-eating plant from *Little Shop of Horrors*, a show I was rehearsing at the time, and which Nicholas referred to as "Little Shop of Horses." He sported green fabric leaves and his head was engulfed in a Venus flytrap-type pod. Neighbours looked at me a little differently after that Hallowe'en. And not with a newfound respect I might add.

Last year, his eighth Hallowe'en, we felt it was time to let him take some responsibility for determining what costume he would wear as opposed to him just agreeing to my ideas, brilliant as they were.

I knew that I couldn't just say, "So, what would you like to be for Hallowe'en this year?" Because that would be too overwhelming for him and he would get frustrated not knowing where to begin. So I guided him to consider ideas from three categories: animals, characters from television, and toys. He chose animals. From there he decided on a bat. No problem. Black balaclava with small pointy ears over his head, black stretch pants and long black sweater, and black garbage bag wings taped under his arms. Perfect.

Now, this Hallowe'en there were two additional elements to consider: we live in a new neighbourhood (although it is just around the corner from our old neighbourhood), and we wanted to give him even more decision-making power over his costume.

The topic first arose when Nicholas walked into the kitchen one late summer day and announced, "Jennifer, I just want to let you know that Hallowe'en will be on a Tuesday this year." I tried not express surprise at his declaration, but calmly walked over to the small calendar I keep in my purse to check his facts, as I have done on numerous occasions, as we don't have any calendars hanging on the walls of our home. I don't know why I was surprised to note that in fact he was right. He always is.

So I seized the opportunity to gently begin discussions about what he might like to be for Hallowe'en, Tuesday 31st of October.

"Um, I'm not sure." I didn't push. A few days later I asked again.

"I want to dress up as the walking man."

I should have known this would happen. His obsession with traffic signals and pedestrian signals (the walking man being the symbol that tells people it is OK to walk) was not something I wanted to indulge, much as I wanted him to choose his own costume. I sighed. I smoothed my way out of that choice by telling him that people might be confused about what he was, and that maybe there was a better choice.

"I could be an airbag and I could make a sign that said: 'Warning death or serious injury can occur. Children twelve and under can be killed by the airbag. The back seat is the safest place for children. Never put a rear-facing child seat in the front. Sit as far back as possible from the airbag. Always use seat belts and child restraints.'"

I smiled weakly at his idea but broadly at his photographic memory. "Yes, I suppose you could do that if you like."

"No, I don't want to. I don't like airbags anymore."

His voice was beginning to pitch up, his jaw was tightening, and his hands were beginning to flap from side to side – he was getting overwhelmed. He started jumping up and down, shaking his hands in agitation.

"I want to be a dead fir tree, not evergreen but everBLACK!"

I calmly suggested he could take some more time to think about it and we could talk about it later. I wondered whether letting him decide was simply too stressful for him. I made a mental note to structure the discussion more carefully next time, maybe even schedule it so he could be prepared.

As Hallowe'en drew nearer, we began to read Hallowe'en stories. I hoped he might get a costume idea from one of them. Instead, we crashed headfirst into that familiar, darned Theory of Mind struggle. The story is one of a boy who takes his little sister out trick or treating and is scared when he sees her going into what all the neighbourhood kids regard as the witch's house. The boy has to go in after his sister but is understandably scared until he realizes that the woman who lives there is not a witch after all but rather an elderly widow woman who has difficulty keeping up the big house. Well, not only does Nicholas want to focus on minute details within the story (like how many leaves are still on the oak branch in the picture) rather than following the arc of the action, but he has real trouble understanding why the boy in the story is afraid of the nice widow woman. I try to explain that the boy doesn't know she is a nice woman until he meets her, but in Nicholas' mind, if Nicholas knows she is a nice lady at the end of the first read-through, then so should the boy in the story. He just cannot assume the perspective of the boy's innocence at the beginning of the story.

A few days later, I informed him that we were going to talk about a Hallowe'en costume after school that day. Later, after homework was done, we sat on the couch and I asked him if he had made a decision about what he wanted to be for Hallowe'en.

"Yes. Geoff Edwards."

Although I was pleased that he actually chose a person instead of an inanimate object this time, my mind raced forward to us arriving on the doorstep of the nice woman across the street and her asking Nicholas politely, "And what are you dressed as?" and Nicholas holding out his treat bag and saying, "Geoff Edwards" and the nice woman across the street saying, "Who?" and Nicholas starting to get frustrated and impatient and yelling, "Geoff Edwards!" and the still nice woman asking, "Geoff Edwards – who is he?" and Nicholas starting to get anxious and through gritted teeth yelling, "He's the host of Treasure Hunt, silly!!!" and her looking apologetically to me, not understanding what she did that upset him so, and me trying to calm him down and remind him, once again, that other people don't have the same information in their heads as he does in his.

I come back to the present and suggest that he might want to think of someone or something else that people would be able to guess, because not everyone gets the Game Show Network.

"A streetlamp!"

With only a few days left until Hallowe'en, I knew we couldn't pull that one off.

"Maybe this year, because we have all been so busy, we might go to the store to choose a costume. After all, Hallowe'en is on Wednesday, and you can't keep changing your mind, which means changing your thoughts to something else."

Explicitly explaining such turns of phrase to his literal mind has become second nature to me.

I hoped that at the store he could see with his own eyes what there was to choose from, and finally make a decision.

Off to the store we drove. Selection was sparse this close to Hallowe'en. "Thank goodness," I mumbled under my breath. I realized my two mistakes at once. One: he can always hear me no matter how softly I speak or how far away I am. Two: the word good is at the top of his list of words he doesn't like people to say. He got agitated. "When you say good, I'd rather you said great."

"Thank greatness there are only a few costumes from which to choose," I corrected myself.

We started at one end of the rack and pulled out possible costumes to consider. Astronaut. Race Car Driver. Clown.

"No way, Jose, I was a clown Saturday, October 31st when I was in grade one."

I put the clown back. Monk. Bam-Bam from the Flintstones. Vampire. He didn't seem excited about any of these. Of course not. They weren't inanimate objects or game show hosts.

There was one lonely costume left at the end of the rack. Little Red Riding Hood.

"Yes! Yes!" he yelled, "I want to dress up as Little Red Riding Hood!"

I could feel a store full of eyes and half smirks descend upon me. My moment of hesitation seemed like an hour, as once again my mind raced forward to him walking around the neighbourhood dressed as Little Red Riding Hood, and the groups of boys from his school we encountered giggling and snickering. On the one hand, he will be totally unaware of the meaning of the snickers; on the other hand, I'm not sure that I should actively set him up for the ridicule. As I hear the snickers of the kids in one ear, I hear him in real time yelling, "Yes, yes, I want to be Little Red Riding Hood and that is my final decision!"

OK. That's it then. I replaced the rejected costumes on the rack, secretly hoping he'd change his mind, which means changing his thoughts to something else. He didn't say anything.

"OK then, let's go pay for it."

The cashier took one look at the front of the package at the pretty little five-year-old girl smiling sweetly from under her adorable little red hood, and then at my excited eight-year-old son, who is so tall he looks more like twelve, and her mouth took on a condescending smile that made my heart sink. Was I making a mistake? No, I reasoned, it was more important to have him make the decision and support it than worry about what others might think. Done.

Hallowe'en night arrives. The night reserved for the walking of ghouls and witches and disembodied spirits. Oh yes, and Little Red Riding Hood.

The jack-o-lanterns are lit. The scary music is put on. The candy is put in a bowl by the front door. Early trick or treaters, tots dressed as lambs and pumpkins, are greeted by a running, yelling Nicholas who opens the door only as much as is necessary to extend handfuls of candy which he drops into open bags. No conversation, no curiosity about who is at his door. He just wants to get it over with. Yes, I am sure we are making a grand impression among our new neighbours.

And to further solidify our reputation, it's time for Nicholas and me to head out to do our trick or treating. He goes upstairs to get on his under-costume: black leggings and a black turtleneck. I take the costume upstairs and we unwrap it and gently unfold the red cape, the red dress, and the white apron. He slips it all over his head. He looks at me wanting me to tie the cape strings under his chin. I try not to smile. He looks hilarious. But a different kind of hilarious from the peanut butter sandwich hilarious. This hilarious is not cute, but instead a tad pathetic, and has more than a little of the British pantomime about it. But his face still holds the same innocence and naivete of the younger peanut butter sandwich days.

We head to the door. I adjust my tiara in the hall mirror, and we're on our way. David looks to me questioningly and mimes clicking a camera. I shake my head no. I don't need that battle, even though I would love a snapshot of this for the photo album. But the cost would be very high indeed, and I want this evening to be a success. Nicholas has not allowed, under any circumstances, his picture to be taken for two years now. When asked why, he gets very distressed and says he doesn't want to talk about it. His refusal to have his picture taken has, on occasion, made him seem to others more like a temperamental movie star than a child with autism.

We say goodbye to David and head down the driveway. "It's moony tonight," Nicholas says, looking up at the full moon. Before I feed him an alternate way of phrasing that sentiment, I take a moment to appreciate the logic from which it stems. If it's sunny during the day, it figures it would be moony at night.

As we walk out of our driveway, I'm apprehensive. We don't know many of the neighbours yet, and I'm torn between introducing and explaining him or just letting things happen and risking a shaky first impression. I decide to let the chips fall where they may.

We walk to the corner and cross the street. He won't deviate from the pedestrian rules of the road that I have taught him, not even for Hallowe'en. I might be grateful for his strict adherence to traffic rules someday.

The first house. He walks boldly up to the front door, knocks and yells, "Trick or Treat." A very nice woman with what seems like a Portuguese accent answers the door and asks him his name. Without looking at her, he mutters, "Nicholas Dana Overton," and thrusts his open treat bag into her door. She tosses in gum and a bag of chips.

"I don't care for gum," he says, and pulls it out of the bag and hands it back to her. He turns and walks toward me. I remind him to say thank you and he turns and yells it. She smiles thinly as she closes the door. So much for first impressions.

As we walk to the next house I coach him on his manners, reminding him to say thank you and to just take what he is given, we can sort it out later.

He does great at the next house. And the next one, and the next one. He's having a good time, although he starts to test me with an inappropriately loud volume for "Trick or Treat."

We meet Josh and Brody, two boys from Nic's class at school. They are dressed as Harry Potter and a robot respectively. We stop and chat, and the boys talk about what goodies they've received so far. As we continue on, I can hear titters.

But the next house belongs to our friends Cara and Peter Schotch. We were greeted by Cara holding the new puppy, Muggins, whom Nic got to pat nervously while Peter stuffed his bag to overflowing with treats. Of his costume, Peter offered, "Very retro." Bless his heart.

Now loaded down so that the candy bag was getting dragged rather than carried, we had only a few places yet to go.

On the walkway to the front door of the next house was a sign that read "Stop Here for Treats." Nicholas wouldn't go any further. He stood there frozen. I coaxed him toward the door. "No, Jennifer. It says stop here for treats." After I explained that the sign meant for us to stop at the house for treats, not stop at the sign, he approached the door and rang the doorbell.

He was getting tired. Whiny and silly. I told him he already had more candy than he could manage to eat in a month and that we could forgo the last house and head on home, but no, Nicholas

The Inflexible would hear nothing of abandoning the route before it was complete.

Of course the last house had a bazillion steps to the front door, and Nicholas' bulging bag of candy slapped against each one all the way up. No longer a sweet Red Riding Hood carrying her basket full of treats to take to Grandmother's house, what met this homeowner was the big bad wolf in a windblown red cape. He banged on the screen door and yelled, "Trick or Treat – c'mon, hurry up!"

I just hope I don't run into that woman at the corner store when I'm not wearing my wig and sunglasses…

With our reputation in our new neighbourhood firmly cemented, we turned and headed for home. Once in the house, he walked right past Dad's questions about where we went and who we saw, and headed for the family room where he dumped his stash of candy on the floor, and began rifling through it to choose the three treats I had promised he could have before bedtime.

From the front hall where I was taking off my clown nose and tiara, I watched him. He was deep in concentration. Lips pursed forward, sorting candy into piles. His red cape draped over his shoulders, hood back. My Little Red Riding Hood. I took a mental snapshot.

And then the doorbell rang, and teenagers yelled, "Boo!" and cackled with satisfaction. And I saw Nic visibly jump and tense, and flap his hands in anguish. I turned to the door and laughed with the teens that they "got me good," and handed out bags of potato chips and cans of pop into their hungry pillow case bags.

As I turned back to Nicholas, it dawned on me. Why he doesn't see Hallowe'en as a fun day. Why he gets no pleasure in being scared. Why he doesn't delight in the adrenalin rush of a good "Boo!" from an unseen goblin.

It's because every day is Hallowe'en for him. Whereas we relish the unexpected for one day of the year, he lives three hundred and sixty-five of them. His nervous system must be bombarded by sounds and other stimuli every waking moment. He must function at fight or flight response readiness all the time. I could feel my heart pounding after the scare from the teenagers at the door – for him it must have been like a rhinoceros thundering toward him.

I resist the urge to go to him and hug him, as I imagine it must feel to him like being suffocated and tortured. My Little Red Riding Hood. Not so little.

I approach him slowly and ask if he's decided which candy he's going to have.

We sit and talk quietly while he eats, and thankfully no one comes to the door. We gather up the rest of his haul and put it in the pantry for subsequent days. I ask him if he would like to wear his costume to bed. "No, that's not allowed," he chastises me. I tell him that I was just teasing.

As he heads up the stairs in his red cape, I call to him and blow him a kiss. He blows one back. Another Hallowe'en under his belt. Or apron.

Just three hundred and sixty-four left to go this year.

November 11th: Remembrance Day

Lest We Forget

Remembrance Day is a day to stop and reflect. To remember those who have gone before. To acknowledge our debt to those who have fought the good fight so that the lives of future generations could be better. A day to link the past with the present. A day to recognize the contributions of heroes.

Not all heroes have made their contributions on the field of battle. Although the day is meant to mark the debt we owe to their courage, there are other battlefields as well, and some of the battles go on for a lifetime.

Take this Remembrance Day trivia quiz to test your knowledge of four brilliant and courageous "eccentrics" in history, each of whom struggled bravely as they "marched to the beat of a different drummer."

Answers can be found at the end of the quiz.

1. Who was slow to talk; in fact, was not completely fluent even at age nine?

    a.   Picasso

    b.   Einstein

    c.   Andy Warhol

    d.   Glenn Gould

2. Who absolutely hated going to school?

    a.   Glenn Gould

    b.   Einstein

    c.   Picasso

    d.   Andy Warhol

    e.   all of the above

3. Whose teacher said to his father, who had enquired about possible career choices for his son, "It doesn't matter what he chooses to do – he'll never amount to anything, whatever he does."

    a.   Andy Warhol

    b.   Picasso

    c.   Einstein

    d.   none of the above

4. Who reportedly had an extraordinary memory?

    a.   Einstein

    b.   Picasso

    c.   Glenn Gould

    d.   Einstein and Glenn Gould

5. Who had sensory issues?

    a.   Picasso

    b.   Glenn Gould

    c.   Einstein

    d.   all of the above

6. In childhood, and as an adult, who was considered "isolated," a loner, not being interested in socializing with peers, or comfortable in social situations?

    a.   Glenn Gould

    b.   Einstein

    c.   Andy Warhol

    d.   all of the above

7. Who was considered extremely visual in his approach to things?

    a.   Picasso

    b.   Einstein

    c.   Andy Warhol

    d.   all of the above

8.   Who admitted to liking animals better than people?

    a.   Picasso

    b.   Glenn Gould

    c.   Andy Warhol

    d.   all of the above

9.   Who was able to perform two mental functions at once?

    a.   Einstein

    b.   Glenn Gould

    c.   Picasso

    d.   Andy Warhol

10.   Who was considered a "pack rat"?

    a.   Glenn Gould

    b.   Andy Warhol

    c.   Einstein

    d.   Picasso

11. Who is credited with saying that he had been able to develop his theories because as a child he had been intellectually retarded and therefore came to matters like time and space in adulthood and approached them with an innocence and naivete?

    a. Einstein

    b. Glenn Gould

    c. Picasso

    d. Andy Warhol

12. Who said, "We must not only tolerate differences between individuals and between groups, but we should indeed welcome them and look upon them as enriching our existence."

    a. Einstein

    b. Andy Warhol

    c. Picasso

    d. Glenn Gould

Trivia Quiz Answers

1 b. Einstein. It was said that he would construct and mutter whole sentences before uttering a word.

2 e. All of the above. Stories abound about all of these geniuses having to be dragged screaming to school. Apparently Picasso couldn't concentrate early on in his studies, but spent his school days drawing compulsively and occasionally going to the

window, tapping it repeatedly. Einstein was considered a slow learner and backward.

3 c.   Einstein, who showed no early signs of his brilliance.

4 d.   Einstein and Glenn Gould. Einstein had instant recall of any scientific fact, even in his later years, and yet could not recall much from his childhood. Glenn Gould had an astounding musical memory, rarely needing to read music, even at a very young age.

5 d.   All of the above. Einstein is reported to have been fascinated by the reflection of light on water and spinning objects, watching them for hours. Picasso's parents were concerned about his intense fascination with textures as a small child. Gould was very sensitive auditorily, both loving to attend to the fading vibration of certain piano sounds as a young child, and also able to distinguish between almost identical sounds. He had perfect pitch.

6 d.   All of the above have been described this way. In fact, Glenn Gould in adult life was noted to actively avoid people, crossing streets and retreating in hallways to avoid encounters. Early in his career he ceased performing live, preferring to play in the isolation of a recording studio. Einstein maintained a wide-eyed innocence and wonder in interview situations. Andy Warhol preferred to observe his notorious parties from another room.

7 d.   All of the above. Picasso apparently had early difficulty with mathematics, as he perceived them as forms rather than concepts. For instance, he saw a seven as an upside-down nose, a three as sideways buttocks, etc. He was drawing at a very early age. Andy Warhol had acute visual memory. It is said that Einstein's visual imagination allowed him to formulate the Theory of Relativity; in fact, his brain was later discovered to have enhanced areas of mathematical and visual/spatial activity, perhaps as compensation for a noted lack in the parietal operculum.

8 b.   Glenn Gould. In fact, he spoke of one day wanting to open an animal shelter designed to house any and all stray dogs in order

to save them from destruction. By contrast, he claimed that people always disappointed him.

9 b.   Glenn Gould. Apparently, he could memorize music while having a conversation, listen to two radios at once, and read while talking on the telephone.

10 a. Glenn Gould and b. Andy Warhol. Upon his death, executors found room upon room of shopping bags filled with purchases never opened in Andy Warhol's apartment. Glenn Gould's friends were in constant amazement at the amount of clutter that filled his home.

11 a. Einstein

12 a. Einstein

December 25th: Christmas

A Visit to Oma's

A m I insane? I hang up the phone. I guess so. Yes, definitely lost my mind. I have just informed my mother that we will be coming for Christmas. For ten days. Call the loony bin – I'm on my way!

It's not that I don't love my family, or that I don't want to see them. I do. That is not the issue. Far from it. The issue is that a cross-country trip during the holiday season is stressful in and of itself, but add an autistic child to the mix and the stressometer… well, its numbers don't go that high. A Christmas trip to Grandma's house? Oma's house in our case. What have I done?!

I can call back and renege. But she was so thrilled. How naive of her. Had she forgotten our last visit? The disastrous long weekend last year, the first time he had been home with me since his diagnosis? Did she really not remember my sister's party, when he pressed his head between my knees and screamed at the top of his lungs when everyone sang Happy Birthday, then raced over to the table and knocked the entire chocolate fudge cheesecake – my sister's favourite – to the floor? Or the next day when one of his young cousins unwittingly got too close, and my son put his hands around his unsuspecting neck?

I remember. The emotional rollercoaster. The frustration and embarrassment about his strange behaviour. The heartache at seeing his autism so starkly contrasted against my 'normal' family. Catching those glimpses of pity in my siblings' eyes. All weekend I had fought the impulse to run into my mother's arms. I was afraid that if I gave in, I would never stop crying.

Even reliving the pain of that weekend, I don't pick up the phone to cancel our plans. No matter what the emotional cost, he should know his extended family. And I miss them. I'm homesick. The holiday season beckons.

We have all grown a lot in the past year. Maybe I am even ready to be held in my mother's arms, and not be consumed by grief.

And so the weeks of preparation begin. First, I email siblings and lay some ground rules:

- Respect his sensory sensitivities.
- Don't approach him quickly.
- Never extend a hand to him or try to hug him.
- Don't crowd him.
- Talk quietly to him.
- Avoid sudden loud noises or warn him that they are coming.
- When we come to your house, please allocate a room where he can go when he feels overstimulated.

I balance my fear of seeming demanding and overbearing with the realization that they will appreciate some concrete ideas on how to avoid a repeat of the last visit.

Having prepared those on the other end, I begin working on the home front.

Nicholas is a visual learner and reads way above age level, so I make calendars with our itinerary written in. I write stories about our upcoming trip: who we will see, where he will sleep, the plane ride, where and how Santa is going to find him at Oma's house. We role-play, and act out scripts that are aimed at giving him strategies to deal with potentially problematic situations and reduce his anxiety. Our house is plastered with pictures, calendars and stories about our upcoming holiday trip.

The day for departure arrives. I pack carefully. His most comfortable clothes. Check. His most beloved toys and books. Check. Everything possible to reduce his stress level. His hand-held electronic Wheel of Fortune game is a must for the plane. Check. I don't care if it drives the other passengers crazy – believe me, if they knew the alternative, they would thank me. Head phones. Check. Favourite snacks. Check. OK. Had I done everything? Oops, pack those social stories and an erasable calendar. Check.

OK. Across the river and into the woods, to Oma's house we go...

I try not to show my nervousness. What if he shrieks or tantrums in the airport or on the plane? I half consider pinning a sign to his back that reads I CAN'T HELP IT – I'M AUTISTIC. Nah – let people think that bad parenting is the cause of his behaviour if they want to.

We board the plane, my son wearing his noise reduction headphones. The stewardess sweetly asks, "Something wrong with his ears?" I open my mouth to explain his auditory sensitivity and processing difficulties, but opt to just smile and say "Yes." As we walk down the aisle toward our seats, a crisp steward nods knowingly and leans down and asks Nicholas innocently, "What radio station are you listening to?" Again, I smile, and usher Nic along.

When we are seated, my son asks, "Stewardess, may I have one pillow, or a combination of two pillows?" She looks at him oddly. I guess she doesn't watch The Price is Right, where one spin or a combination of two spins earns you a prize, and unlike my son, she doesn't perceive the world through the lens of his favourite game show. She hands him two pillows. I quietly remind him to say thank you. "Thank you, Stewardess. You are the grand prize winner!" She moves down the aisle to tend to someone a little less disconcerting.

We arrive at Oma's house, the plane trip having been relatively uneventful. Thank goodness. But we can't relax yet. We have entered the woods. We are in the thick of the woods. But we are by no means out of the woods yet.

Each of the ten days we are there, we spend a great deal of time preparing him for upcoming events, and guiding him through difficult times. It isn't easy.

And he has his meltdown moments, but with quiet coaching they don't last long.

Yes, I have more than one pang of resentment at seeing my siblings with their comparatively easy children.

Yup, my heart pinches to see three of his cousins on the floor in a cousin sandwich, and my son in the corner, oblivious to their infectious giggling.

And no question that he is autistic. His greeting upon entering everybody's house is, "Do you have the Game Show Network?" and then he lists all the hosts of all the game shows, and recites the entire twenty-four hour Game Show Network schedule. Sure, this is embarrassing, but on the other hand, they are amazed to see him, a kid in kindergarten, creating Wheel of Fortune puzzles with their scrabble tiles and playing out the game.

And he makes us laugh. One evening at my sister's he declares: "I don't like my dinner, unfortunately. I'm ready for some dessert now."

The big day – Christmas Day – the busiest, noisiest, longest day of the visit starts off bumpy.

The night before he had carefully placed the traditional plate of cookies and jigger of scotch for Santa and the carrots for the reindeer by Oma's fireplace. He adjusted things eight times before the arrangement met with his satisfaction. I prayed he wouldn't look too closely and realize that Oma's fireplace was in fact propane and consequently there was no chimney for old Saint Nick to come down. Thankfully he didn't.

He then wrote his note to Santa:

> Dear Santa
>
> I want a Candyland game and a Candyland computer game.
>
> Love Nicholas Dana Overton

He placed his note beside the goodies on the hearth, then went willingly to bed in Oma's guestroom, and quickly fell asleep.

Christmas morning. He wakes up, but he won't leave the room without us. In the few minutes it takes David and me to wipe the sleep from our eyes and get ready to accompany him, Nicholas gets increasingly overexcited and transforms into a pacing, hand-flapping ball of tension, bombarding us with questions and concerns about Santa's ability to find Oma's house.

We are all relieved to reach the living room and find the carrots and scotch consumed, a message from Santa scribbled at the bottom of Nic's note to him, and a stack of gifts.

Knowing he is already on the fast track to meltdown, we try to keep the excitement level down while stockings and gifts are being opened. Our voices are kept low; wrapping paper is slowly removed, and 'Oooohs' and 'Ahhhs' kept to a minimum.

I desperately want to avoid triggering his love/hate relationship with new toys.

He opens his Candyland computer game from Santa. His eyes open wide. Then he throws it across the room. "I hate Christmas. I don't like this. Let's sell it at a yard sale. I want to hurt Santa's feelings."

I shoot a look at my mother. She heeded my coaching well. She simply ignores what he said and avoids eye contact with him while we redirect him to something else.

Time for a break. Time for breakfast. When he is not looking I place his opened gifts out of the way until he is ready to approach them on his terms. Maybe not for a few days.

While we eat, I pray that this morning isn't an indication of what the rest of the day will be like. Please, not on Christmas. Not in front of my entire family.

After breakfast, we make our way to my brother's house. As we approach the front door, I smile nervously at my son and encourage him to ring the doorbell.

I take a deep breath, and remind myself to take some time to stop worrying about Nicholas, and simply enjoy my family.

Amidst the chaos of the day, as events and people go spinning around him, he is definitely the grand prize winner.

I am so proud of him. He quietly excuses himself when things get too much. He remembers to say "you're too close" when a younger child runs up to him. He and I share secret looks across the room of "I did it" and "You did it!"

And he amazes us when he plays hide and seek with one of his cousins! No prompting, no cues. Spontaneous. So what if he places his cousin into the hiding place and then covers his eyes to count – he is playing with another child and loving it! "Let's do it again!" he shouts. I simply beam. Speechless, wanting desperately to hug him. But I can't. So I am content to quietly beam, and give him lots of verbal praise.

There is a palpable sigh in the room. We all relax and celebrate the occasion and ourselves.

The next day is the day to leave and go back home to Halifax. And my child, the child who had been so anxious about the visit; the child who had been frantic about sleeping somewhere different; this same child suddenly doesn't want to leave! "When will I come back to Oma's house?" he insists. And before I can answer, he states, "I think maybe Friday." Sweetheart. Today is Wednesday.

As we stand at the door saying our goodbyes, my autistic son runs up to my mother and gives her a hug. "Goobye, Oma." We all blink back a tear.

Now it's my turn to hug my mother. I walk, not run, into her arms. Smiling, not crying. She whispers how proud she is of me. We stand in a long embrace, our damp cheeks pressed together.

The three of us turn and walk out the door, on the way back to Halifax and our life. All of us stronger for this journey.

We have gone over the river and through the woods, and out the other side. Safely to Oma's house.

The way seems clearer now. Not as scary. We can make this journey again.

January 1st: New Year's Day

Please Stand By

New Year's Day. A day of transition. A brief pause between the hectic pace of the holiday season and the bustle of the coming year. A day to lounge in pajamas, eat leftovers on the couch, and read. A day to discourage visits and avoid leaving the house at all costs. "Hanging out," as Nicholas calls it. A day of quiet reflection. To contemplate the successes and failures of the past year. And to make plans for the coming year.

Mid afternoon finds the three of us huddled around the woodstove in the family room. On the coffee table sits a bowl of half-eaten popcorn, glasses with a few ice cubes resting at the bottom, and a just-finished game of Snakes and Ladders.

"I'm the grand prize winner!" Nicholas yells as he runs through the house, and to the computer to play with his Christmas gift: a computer version of Wheel of Fortune featuring the real Vanna White!

Dinner is a faraway thought. The perfect time to grab a piece of paper and pencil from the messy coffee table and sit back in the chair closest to the fire, and turn my thoughts to the year behind us and the year ahead. And to formulate some resolutions.

David gets up and heads to the front door, mumbling about the snowstorm. The only thing that could get him to head outside today would be the television, of course. The satellite dish is on the blink because of the storm. He heads downstairs to grab his homemade satellite-dish-snow-cleaner-off-er. More mumbling. I hear the front door blow shut behind him. Perfect. I nudge my chair closer to the fire, and confront the blank piece of paper in front of me.

So. What would I like to accomplish this year? I put pencil to paper.

Lose twenty pounds.

Exercise three times a week.

Read a book a month.

Eat better.

Reduce stress.

Catalogue a systematic approach for teaching Nicholas skills.

Make more money.

Be more patient.

…My thoughts are interrupted as Nicholas comes skipping into the family room with his arms in the air, "I'm the grand prize winner a second time!!!" He runs toward me and I think for a minute that he might actually run into my arms to share his excitement. I should have known better. He stops in front of me and asks, "May I talk to you or do you have to concentrate?" This phrase was cute the first time I heard it. But I hear it a hundred times a day. I attempt to hide the weariness in my voice as I answer, "No, you can talk to me."

"Can I read this or is it private?" This phrase often accompanies the previous one.

"Sure go ahead, buddy."

He glances at the paper. "Why do you need to lose twenty pounds?"

"Because I'm too fat."

"Do you have to spell fat F-A-T or can it be spelled P-H-A-T, or G-H-A-T like in laugh?" and, not waiting for an answer, he's off again for another round of his victory dance.

"What are you going to do now?" I ask, trying to focus him.

"I think I'll make a phone call. I think I'll call that woman on the phone that tells me to hang up and try my call again."

Gentle redirection required.

"Maybe you'd like to make a list too," I suggest. "I'm making a list of things I'd like to do this year; why don't you make a list of three things you'd like to do?" I've learned to be specific and clear to help frame the activity.

"OK." He grabs a piece of paper and pencil from the table in front of the window and sets to work. Another few moments of peace and quiet. I should have suggested he write seventeen things he would like to do. After all, seventeen is his favourite number.

I review what I have written so far. It bears a striking resemblance to the list I wrote last year at this time. And the year before that. Hmmmm.

David's going to laugh at me when he comes inside. He is not a resolution-making kind of person. He is more the live-life-day-to-day kind of person. I'm a nut about punctuality. He is late for everything. I tend to be goal oriented. David's more interested in the process of getting there. I make things happen. He lets things happen. Me Type A. He Type B. I know he's going to laugh at me when he comes inside...

I hear the wind suddenly pick up. Or is it just David's muffled cursing from outside?

I check in with Nic. "How is your list coming?"

"Why is it snowing? Did Uncle George open a cloud?" Uncle George died five years ago, and I guess Nicholas figures he's up in heaven orchestrating the weather.

Gentle redirection. "How is your list?"

"I'm finished."

I have to ask if I can look at it because he has no instinct to show off his work.

He hands it to me a little too firmly. One of his many testing behaviours. I shoot him a look of warning.

I look at what he has created. He skips away, singing the Twelve Days of Christmas: "FIIIIIVVVE GOLDEN RINGS!"

To Do

1. call car dealership re: cars

2. call Vanna re: turning vowels

3. call Santa re: presents

He's obviously modeled his list on one of my many lists that litter the house. I call out to him, "Why do you need to talk to Santa about presents?"

"I want to tell him what I want next Tuesday December 25th," comes the reply from the kitchen. How does he know next Christmas will fall on a Tuesday?! But it doesn't surprise me any more. This morning David ceremoniously unwrapped the new calendar for the year, but before hanging it in the kitchen, David held the calendar away from Nic, and quizzed him on what day of the week special occasions will fall on this year. Without having to think, he guessed them all right. Intrigued and a little freaked out, David then asked questions about years past and out of sequence. Nic answered quickly, and David checked his responses on my palm pilot, which holds a ten-year calendar in its memory. Nic scored one hundred percent!

I call to him, "I like your list, Nicholas." I get up to stoke the fire.

Grabbing another log from the fireside, I realize he has come a long way in the four years since his diagnosis.

Four years ago there was much less language, let alone conversation.

Three years ago he could read and spell like a whiz, but didn't always comprehend at the same level as he was reading.

Two years ago I would have to say his name before speaking to him or else he wouldn't know I was talking to him.

And a year ago, it would have been like pulling teeth to get him to sit down and complete a task independently.

As intense as the past few years have been, they have flown past. I guess it's true that time goes faster as you get older. My mother warned me about that.

A twinge of panic in my solar plexus.

Does that mean that tomorrow I will wake up and he'll be eighteen? An adult in the eyes of society? And will he be as developmentally uneven as he is today, only taller and with a deeper voice?

Will he have finished high school by then or will he have struggled academically and been held back a year or more? Will he have been bullied in high school? Will he have even known he was being bullied? Will he be able and interested in attending university or a community college?

Will he have ambitions for the future? Will he be going off to meet friends at a local coffee shop?

Will he harbour any desire for independence? Will he be functional enough to live independently?? Will he have a driver's license? Will he be able to manage money?

Will he still get frustrated at simple tasks like tying his shoelace? Will he still be able to easily recall minute details from long ago, yet have to refer to a 'How To' sequence list when brushing his teeth? Will he ever care if his shirt is on backwards?

Will he be labeled and given up on by those around him? Will he be stigmatized? Will he have a job? Will he require and be eligible for a disability pension?

Will his obsessions turn into career opportunities?

Will he be happy?

Will he still cover his ears at the sound of running water? Will he still wear his noise reduction headphones?

Will he be interested in establishing a meaningful relationship with another human being? Will he still hate to be touched? How will his sexuality express itself?

Will he still make charts and compile detailed information about birds or botany? Will he still sing obscure Broadway show tunes? Will he still be drawing street lamps and traffic signals?

Will he still be highly anxious about walking into a store because the floor might be damp and he might slip and fall?

Will he still fly into a rage when someone says a word he doesn't like? Will he still interrogate people about their family trees? Will he still retain all that information?

Will he still flap his hands when excited?

Will he still be as handsome as he is today?

So many unanswered questions. And will there ever be answers?

Is this year going to be the year when the cause of autism is discovered? Will this year bring some further understanding of the disorder? Will there be an explanation for the startling rise in the number of diagnoses? Will we learn which genetic factors are present? Will environmental considerations such as food sensitivities and vaccinations be determined to contribute to the disorder?

Will there finally be some willingness and ability to go beyond the broad, catch-all diagnosis of Autism Spectrum Disorder or Pervasive Developmental Disorder, to clarify how this disorder actually manifests itself, what parts of my son's brain are affected, and exactly how his brain functions differently from ours?

Will I ever understand how he perceives the world?

Will anyone ever tell us what we can expect in terms of his adult functioning level?

Will there be someone to care for him, understand him, and love him should something happen to David and me?

Feeling impatient and angry, I take it out on the logs in the wood stove, poking them into submission.

I close the stove door and turn to head back to my chair.

As I turn, I see Nicholas, standing beside the television. Staring straight ahead of him, his face neutral.

"What are you doing sweetie?" I venture.

"I'm standing by."

Before I can open my mouth to ask what he means, I get it. I look to the television screen. It is blank but for a thin blue band running along the bottom which reads "Please Stand By. Searching for Satellite Signal."

I look to Nicholas. His totally serious face makes me want to laugh and cry at the same time. I want to laugh in recognition and appreciation of the way his literal mind translates the world around him. But I also want to cry at the implications of his naivete. So much goes on in this world that is not explicit. So much human communication depends on nuance and ambiguity. Will he ever understand? Would he go jump in the lake if someone told him to, like the guy in the film The Manchurian Candidate?

My heart is breaking. I stare into the fire.

No. I don't want him to have to grow up and go out into that world, that world that he won't understand and that won't understand him the way we do. I want to harbour him here in our safe haven. I don't want him to grow up. I want time to stay frozen, as frozen as the ground outside. Is that so wrong?

Deep in my heart, I know it is.

I know that the coming year will bring more of this balancing act we've been practising for the past four years. The balance of letting him be who he is AND working to prepare him for what he needs to know.

More balancing our cautiously optimistic hopes for his future with a healthy dose of "realistic" thrown into the mix. Without any answers. One day at a time.

I look over to Nicholas, and say gently to him, "Nicholas, 'please stand by' does not mean you have to stand by the television. It's an expression people sometimes say. It means wait and see what happens."

"I see." He doesn't move.

"So you don't have to stand there."

"OK." He relaxes his posture and runs into the other room.

I resume my seat and review my resolutions list. Time to balance optimism with a little reality here as well. Inject a little Type B into my Type A.

I cross out what I have written. Beside the crossed out list I write:

Drink more water.

Walk daily.

Read one book not related to autism.

Revise our will.

Hang out more with my son.

A cold gust of air as David walks in and shakes the snow off his head, and leans the satellite-dish-snow-cleaner-off-er against the wall.

"I'm not having much luck out there. Has the signal returned on the television or does it still say 'Please Stand By'?"

"I'm afraid so. No signal yet. C'mon inside and get warm. We'll just have to wait and see what happens."

February 14th: Valentine's Day

Roses Are Red

★★★★★★★

"Homework time, buddy!"

"Is it three-thirty?"

"Yes, it's exactly three-thirty. Time for homework."

"Can I finish what I'm doing or does it have to stop?"

"Finish your game, and then we'll do homework. In the family room. I'll go set it up."

★★★★★★★

"OK. Here's what we're going to do today. Do you want me to write it out for you?"

"No. I'll remember."

"OK. First we're going to write a Valentine's Day poem. Tomorrow is Valentine's Day, remember?"

"What's second?"

"Then you are going to write your valentines for your school friends. Then we are going to look at this sheet of emotions. So, that's three things we're going to do for homework today. So, what's the first thing we're going to do?"

"Valentine's Day poem. Can you sit over there or do you need to stand too close to me? You're too close!"

"Nicholas, remain calm. I need to show you what to do, and then I'll move away, OK?"

"I don't like it when you stand too close to me."

"OK. The poem. Here are the first two lines that Ms. Ferguson has sent home."

"You mean 'to the house' – don't say 'home'! When you say home, I'd rather you said 'to the house'."

"These are the two lines that Ms. Ferguson has given you, and now you have to write two more lines to finish the poem.

> *Roses are red.*
> *Violets are blue.*

"Now think of two more lines. Remember, the last word of the fourth line has to rhyme with 'blue'. So, like: Roses are red, violets are blue, sugar is sweet, and so are you. But you make up your own two lines. What do you think you would like your poem to say?"

> *"Roses are red*
> *Violets are blue*
> *A porkchop is brown*
> *Wrens are too."*

"That's great – I love it!"

"Be embarrassed – I don't want you to be proud."

"All right, I'm very embarrassed – you did a great job. So write that down in your homework book, and while you do that, I'll get your valentine cards 'cause that's what we're going to do next, right?"

"Yes. Jennifer, if the pencil lead is grey, I can ask for a younger pencil with a dark lead."

"You can choose whichever pencil you want. Now write that poem in your book."

"I'm not ready!"

"Nicholas..."

"I don't want you to lose your patience. I want you to keep it!"

"OK. Let's both keep our voice volume low, and concentrate on the poem."

"What time will we be finished – four colon three zero?"

"Yup. If you get started we will be done homework by four-thirty."

"Then can we play Hangman?"

"Sure."

★★★★★★★

"Super job, Nic. Now do you want the class list so you know which kids' names to write on your valentines?"

"No. I know it. I remember from when Ms. Ferguson takes attendance."

"OK. And what are you going to write?"

"To Adam Amberson. Love Nicholas Dana Overton."

"Do the boys in your class write the word 'love' when writing valentines to the other boys in the class?"

"Yes they do, yes they do!"

"OK then. But I think it would be more appropriate to say 'From Nicholas Dana Overton' instead of 'Love Nicholas Dana Overton' when you are writing a valentine to a boy. Let's practise that. Here are the valentines. You get started. I'm just going over here to put another log on the fire. It's cold in here."

"Jennifer, when I was six and I objected to sitting in the back seat of the car, did I support sitting in the front seat?"

"Nic, valentines please."

"Dad said support is the opposite of object."

"Valentines."

"An announcement. Please vehicles, no turning right on St. Margaret's Bay Road. Thank you. Another announcement. Please people, no shopping at the Price Club. Shop somewhere else. Thank you."

"Nicholas, shall I come over and help you with your valentines?"

"No. I'll remember to think things but not say them."

"You should be thinking about your valentines right now. Concentrate please, or I'll come and help you do them."

"No! I can do it!!!"

"OK. Show me how you do it."

★★★★★★★

"Jennifer? Say yes dear."

"Yes dear."

"Jennifer, is the cover of my math book hard because the questions in it are difficult?"

"No. Hard can mean two different things. It can mean the opposite of soft – like your book cover; or it can mean difficult – like some of your math questions. Two different meanings for the same word, spelled the same."

"Jennifer, is school work in French 'école travail'?"

"Yes, probably. Dad will know for sure. Which name are you writing on that valentine?"

"Amber Tortelli."

"Great – you're almost done. How many more?"

"Four more. Wheel of Fortune! Let's meet the contestants. My name is Ms. Horsefall. I work at Nicholas' school."

"Nic."

"I have to mute the TV. What did you say, Jennifer?"

"What TV?"

"The TV in my head."

"Focus please and finish your cards."

"Un-mute the TV. My name is John Dartt. I used to work at Neptune Theatre. My name is Brad Benson. I bully a lot. Let's spin the Wheel! The category is phrase."

"Nicholas Overton! Who is the next person on your class list? Do I have to come and sit beside you?"

"No! No! I can do it!"

★★★★★★★

"OK. All done. Super job."

"Be embarrassed!"

"Where shall we sit to look at the emotions list?"

"On the couch. You sit on the middle cushion. I'll sit here. Put your feet under the afghan! You're too close! Jennifer, could Point Pleasant Park be called Point Affable Park? Pleasant means the same as affable."

"You're right. OK. Are we ready to look at this? Some of them are easy and some are difficult for you. Emotion homework is really important for us to practise, so that you can learn what people are feeling. Are you ready?"

"Yes. Jennifer, is the opposite of manure, manolder?"

"No, Nicholas, manure is not spelled M-A-N-E-W-E-R, it's spelled M-A-N-U-R-E, and it's another word for animal poop. A lot of people put manure on their gardens to help the plants grow better. Farmers put it on their fields to help their plants grow too. Now, are we ready to concentrate on this list of emotions?"

"Yes. C'mon on down, you're the next contestant on The Price is Right!"

"Nic. Now, there are a lot of different emotions on this page, let's cover up all the rows except the top row so that we can focus on just these ones. And I'm going to cover up the words so that we can try to guess the emotion by just looking at the faces."

"Are we going to do easy ones or difficult ones?"

"We'll start with the easy ones and then talk about some of the other ones. So. The first one here is, what?"

"Sad."

"Right. How did you know he is sad?"

"He's crying."

"Right. What makes you sad?"

"When people say words and numbers I don't like."

"What is this next one?"

"Happy."

"Right. How did you guess that?"

"He's smiling."

"Right. What makes you happy?"

"Game shows."

"Anything else? I know that working in the garden makes me happy. What are two things that you do that you enjoy and make you happy?"

"Acting out game shows. Looking at the bird book."

"Right. What is this boy feeling? Look at his face."

"Mad."

"He sure is. What's something that makes you mad, or angry?"

"When Wheel of Fortune is not on. When it's a holiday Monday."

"Yeah. Let's move on to the next row. Look at this girl's face and tell me what she's feeling."

"I'm not sure."

"Look at her face. Her eyebrows are up high; her eyes are wide open, and her mouth is wide open."

"I don't know. I'm getting frustrated!"

"I think she's surprised. Something unusual has happened and she is surprised. Like when Dad came home, I mean to the house, and told me he was taking me out for dinner tomorrow night for

Valentine's Day, remember? When he told me that, my eyes got big and my eyebrows went up, and my mouth fell open. I was surprised. And happy too. But first I was surprised."

"Yeah."

"OK. This next one is tough. Look at his face. His hair is straight up, his eyes are big, his eyebrows are high, and his jaw is very tight or tense."

"Scared."

"Yes, that's right, buddy. Name something that scares you."

"Loud noises."

"Yes, that's right. Rollercoasters scare me. This next one looks kind of happy."

"He is happy."

"Well, yes he is. But it's a certain kind of happy. Look at the word."

"Confident. What does confident mean?"

"Well, it means that you feel sure that you are going to do a great job. Like you feel confident before a spelling test, because you know you are going to get all the words right. Yes? It means feeling sure."

"Are we done yet – it's almost four-thirty."

"Let's do three more, and then we'll be done."

"Vanna's barking – go tell her to be quiet."

"I'll do that, and then I'll come back and we'll do three more, OK?"

"Yes. Why is she barking? Is someone walking close to our house or is she caught in her tether? Do you have to hit her with a newspaper? Hit her with a newspaper!"

"I'm just going to tell her to stop barking."

"Will you tell her in a firm volume? Will your voice be black?"

"I'll be right back."

★★★★★★★

"Jennifer, when Vanna barks her head off will she have a stump there?"

"Nic, barking her head off means that she is barking a lot, not that her head is going to fall off. Now back to these emotions. Here's an interesting one: jealous. Do you know what jealous is?"

"No."

"It's when someone has something you want. They have it and you don't. When that happens you are jealous of that person."

"Like when Uncle Bill was bringing Janelle her salad and she wanted it and Uncle Bill was slow bringing it to her."

"Well no, more like if Josh had a really cool Nintendo© game that you wanted but we didn't have enough money to buy it. You would be jealous of Josh because he has the cool Nintendo© game and you don't."

"I see."

"Have you ever felt jealous of someone because they had something you wanted to have?"

"No."

"Next one. How is he feeling?"

"Sad."

"Yes, I think you're right. But why is he sad?"

"Maybe his bicycle broke. Maybe he lost his cat."

"I think he's sad because he's lonely. What does lonely mean?"

"It means alone."

"Yes, that's right. But it means more than alone. It means being sad because you are alone. It means missing the people you love and want to be with. Sometimes we are happy to be alone, but sometimes we feel lonely because we want to be with people and wish those people were here with us. We miss them. That's when we feel lonely."

"I miss Vanna White and Pat Sajack when it's a holiday Monday."

"I know. Do you miss me when I'm at the university or at the theatre?"

"Yes."

"And I miss you too. I feel lonely. And I want to get back here to see you."

"I prefer to be alone."

"Yes, I know you do dear. Last one. Are you ready to guess this one?"

"And then I'll go play Super Mario for seventeen minutes."

"That's fine. Here we go. What is this girl feeling?"

"I'm not sure. Let me read the word! Lovestruck. What does lovestruck mean?"

"Look at the word. Love-struck. It means to be hit by love. Not like someone hitting you with their hands, but that love hits you – you are hit in your heart by the emotion of love. So, you love someone so much that it feels like your heart has been hit by the love that you feel. Does that make sense?"

"No."

"When I tell you I love you, I'm saying that to let you know that I think you are a great kid, that I enjoy being with you, and I want to be with you a lot. Right? I love Dad too. Love is what Valentine's Day is about. People who love each other make cards and buy presents for the people they love. That's why Dad is taking me out for dinner tomorrow night. And that's why I'm making Dad's favourite dinner tonight, and that's why I made heart-shaped cookies for you and your class. And that's why you made me and Dad that very cool card at school. And that's why you give valentines to the kids in your class. To let them know that you like them and enjoy spending time with them."

"And Ms. Williams and Ms. Ferguson too."

"Right. Love means you really, really like someone."

"Am I finished with my homework now? It's four-thirty."

"Yup, that's it for today. We'll talk about these some more tomorrow. I love you."

"I love Super Mario! See you later alligator!"

"In a while crocodile."

Happy Valentine's Day, sweetie...

> *Roses are red,*
> *Violets are blue,*
> *Who's the love of my life?*
> *That would be you.*

February 27th: Grandpa's Birthday

Grandpa's Story

Granpa's Story:
once Upon a time there was a Man
named Dana Herding Overton.
Dana is 82 years Old. That's
Quite old.
Dana lives in an apartment in Vancou
ver. Dana IS David's Father. And
He is my Grandfather.
June is Dana's Wife And it's
Toobad She Died.
Helen is Dana's Friend.
Dana likes to iron.

His favourite Shows are Whose
Line and Jep. There Last Visit
there were Pictures of Dana and
Helen. Dana Has a Brother
Bill and His Family died.
And aunt Kathy is
His sister in Law.

My Birthday

The Gift

Lucky for me, my fortieth birthday fell on a Saturday. I awoke to the strains of Happy Birthday to You, sung by David and Nicholas. They carried balloons and a steaming cup of tea. From behind his back, Nicholas produced a present, wrapped in shiny silver paper. To match the colour of my hair I guess. How thoughtful of them.

As there was no school bus to rush for, they both came into the bedroom and sat on the side of the bed. Nicholas was excited, and climbed over me, and huddled under the covers, showering me with kisses and repeating, "Happy Birthday, Mommy! Open your present, open your present – I made it for you!"

David reached for the camera.

I took a sip of tea, propped myself up on my pillows, and set in to opening this beautiful gift. I had never seen him so eager to please me before. I desperately wanted to linger over this perfect moment, but Nicholas was so impatient and so excited.

I carefully removed the paper from the box. I opened the box. And there was the most beautiful thing I've ever seen. It was a painted cardboard and Popsicle-stick paperclip holder. Handmade by my son!

It stood four inches tall. Four squares of cardboard, glued together and edged with Popsicle sticks, and in each cardboard square a drawing of our family, each member having a speech balloon coming out of their mouths, with sayings like "Pick a paperclip" and "Need a paperclip, Mom?" Even the dog was pictured offering me a paperclip.

"Do you like it?" Nicholas asked, smiling hopefully.

"Like it? I LOVE it!"

He glowed with satisfaction and pride.

"Thank you so much, Nicholas. I'm going to put that on my desk in the study, and keep all my paperclips in it. For ever and ever. This is the most beautiful paperclip holder I've ever seen. Did anyone help you make it?

"No, I did it my own self," he beamed. Then he threw his arms around me and gushed, "I love you Mommy. Happy Birthday!"

I was overwhelmed. How I had longed for this moment. Hugging my son. We held that hug for what seemed like an hour. I whispered in his ear how much I loved him, and that I was so proud of him for making this present for me, and helping Dad make tea for me.

David snapped what seemed like an entire roll of film during this.

"And now, we are leaving you to fall back asleep for a bit while Nic and I go down to the kitchen and whip up a special birthday breakfast for you. A modest little repast of Eggs Benedict, featuring the authentic Overton homemade hollandaise."

He coaxed Nic away from my side, closed the door behind them, and left me to sip tea, nestle back into my pillows, and close my eyes.

I had the feeling that this was going to be a great day.

An hour or so later, David gently knocked on the door to announce that he had drawn me a bath. He ushered me into the bathroom, and the scent of roses filled the room. The tub was surrounded by lit pillar candles. The bath water was littered with rose petals. I was speechless.

He sexily removed my robe and took my hand and eased me into the bathtub. When I was up to my chin in the fragrant water, he handed me a magazine and closed the door.

"What's Nic doing?" I called after him.

He reopened the bathroom door, and smiled around the edge of it. "Don't worry, he's not going to bother you. He's very busy drawing a picture of you all dressed up in a fancy dress, your birthday suit he calls it. I didn't have the heart to explain to him what that really means."

We shared a Tracy and Hepburn laugh, and he closed the door.

I sighed and slid down into the steaming, fragrant water.

The smell of toasted English muffins wafted under the door.

I got out, dried off, examined my forty-year-old face in the mirror, pleased to see that there was not one wrinkle, got dressed, and went downstairs.

There were David and Nicholas side by side at the kitchen counter, slicing strawberries. Nicholas was placing them on the plates and carrying them ever so carefully to the dining room, to the elaborately set table. The best linen tablecloth. More lit candles. Soft classical music played. The fancy china and cutlery.

I felt like a princess.

I must be dreaming. Or else in a movie of the week.

"You sit here, Mom" announced Nicholas, pulling out the chair for me. My little gentleman.

We sat and ate a brunch fit for royalty. And we laughed. And talked.

As David cleared away the dishes, Nicholas showed me the picture he drew. It was beautiful. Me, my hair grey and my eyes blue, dressed in a fancy ballgown, standing in the garden, holding my new paperclip holder, behind me a vibrant rainbow.

I told him that that drawing was exactly how I felt today.

Then Nicholas asked, "What would you like to do now?" I thought for a moment.

"I know you're going to think I'm crazy, but you know how I love to move furniture around to create different looks. So what I would like to do more than anything right now is rearrange the living room furniture."

"That sounds cool – can I help?" he pleaded.

"Are you sure you won't be upset because things are changed around?"

"No problem."

"OK then. Let's start with the sofa!"

The next two hours were spent in blissful experimentation. First, we placed the couch against the far wall, and the chairs and coffee table grouped around it. No, didn't like that layout.

We then moved the couch against the long wall, and placed the chairs opposite it with the coffee table between them. That was OK, but the rest of the room looked empty.

Next we put the couch on an angle in the corner with the big plant behind it. Nah. People would be fighting branches as they sat down on the couch. Not user friendly.

We pulled the plant out and replaced it with a small plant stand from the dining room, and plopped a small fern on top of that.

"What do you think, Nic?"

"This could work."

I agreed. Yes, a definite possibility. No leaves in hair and yet it filled in the triangular gap behind the couch since it was on an angle. We high-fived each other.

"That's a keeper, Mom."

Now to place the rest of the furniture in support of that corner arrangement.

Just then the doorbell rang.

"I'll get it," Nicholas clamoured. Two of his friends were at the door. They wanted him to come out and play. He looked to me.

"I know it's your birthday, but can I, Mom?"

I smiled warmly. "Sure, honey" I assured him. "You go and have fun. But let me or Dad know if you're going to leave the yard, OK?"

"OK, Mom," embarrassed in front of his friends that he still had to report his whereabouts to his parents. At the age of nine. For gosh sakes.

He tied up his sneakers and threw on his windbreaker and he was gone in a burst of laughter and chatter.

I sauntered into the kitchen where David was washing the kitchen floor, and I leaned down and kissed him on the cheek. "Thanks for the great brunch. You are definitely spoiling me today."

"It's your day." He pecked my cheek and resumed scrubbing.

I made my way to the stereo. I picked out a Ray Charles compact disc and popped it into the player. I turned it up full blast, and returned to my living room furniture.

I surveyed my work so far, and all was good. But one more thing was needed: a side table for the blue chair. I moved one from beside the couch.

Presto. Done. New living room. New feel. Open. Airy. Maybe a dinner party in the near future was in order.

I heard Nic and his friends in the backyard, swinging on the swings and saving the universe from the emperors of evil.

I asked David if it was OK that I took a nap. He saluted me, and I headed up the stairs.

I lay down. My eyes lingered over the still-bare tree tops. My ears titillated by the sounds of my boy outside playing with his friends. A contented smile on my lips. I dozed off into a careless slumber.

"Mom, wake up, wake up – we have to get ready for dinner!" woke me. I opened my eyes.

I felt refreshed and ageless.

"Dinner?" I stammered sleepily.

"Yeah, didn't Dad tell you. We're taking you out to dinner tonight. To Da Marizio's – your favourite! C'mon, get up already!"

Wow. Da Marizio's. Expensive. Elegant. I swung my legs over the side of the bed and made my way to the closet. I'm going to have to come up with something pretty swanky for Da Marizio's. My mind immediately started composing and rejecting possible blouse/skirt combinations. I opened the closet door.

There, wrapped in dry cleaner's filmy plastic, was hanging a new dress. Not just any dress. A NEW dress. Definitely swanky.

I screamed. David and Nic came running to see what was wrong. "How did you manage to do this?" I looked at David with a mixture of astonishment and disbelief.

"Is it OK? Is it your size?" he asked with concern.

"OK??!! OhhhKaaay?! It's fabulous! Thank you so much!!" I covered him with kisses.

Nicholas giggled and blushed.

"Happy birthday, my darling. You deserve it. And so much more." More kisses and hoots of pleasure.

They left me to get gussied up. Moments later, David opened the bedroom door just far enough to set a martini on the dresser, then retreated.

The dress fit beautifully. Silk. Slinky. Flattering on this aging mother body. I felt twenty, not forty.

This day could go on for ever as far as I was concerned.

The earrings being the final touch, I made my entrance into the living room, where my boys were reclining and enjoying the new living room arrangement. Side by side on the couch, they read a book together. They whistled as I entered.

"Wow, Mom, super duper."

"You look smashing, sweetheart."

And I was about to be escorted to the ball.

The boys rushed upstairs to get dressed for dinner.

The phone rang as I drained my martini glass. It was my sister calling from Ontario to wish me a happy birthday. We chatted and laughed. I recounted my fabulous day. I thanked her for calling and signed off just as the boys thumped downstairs. Very impressive. David dressed in a blazer and tie; Nicholas had chosen dress pants and a dress shirt.

We locked up the house, and hopped into the car. Well, not hopped. More like placed ourselves carefully into the car. Turning out of the driveway, the old green stationwagon felt like a Lincoln Continental.

At the restaurant we were led to our table by a woman with long flowing curls and a Hollywood smile. Once seated, I asked Nicholas if he would like to wear his headphones as the restaurant was quite noisy. He said no. He told me he doesn't need them much anymore.

We ordered a cocktail. Nicholas ordered tomato juice. We all perused the menu. Nicholas decided on calamari and a salad. David went for the veal specialty of the house. I realized that I turn forty only once, and decided on the most expensive item on the menu: Salmone Croccante. And wine. Lots of wine.

The three of us sipped our drinks and engaged in easy conversation about the week past and the week coming up, friends, work, and school.

Dinner arrived by trolley and was served by a tuxedoed waiter.

Everything was delicious. The food, the wine, the company.

This was the best birthday ever.

Dessert of course is one of the requirements when turning forty. Decadent and delicious.

When we had drained our coffee cups, I took a moment to thank my two men for their thoughtfulness and planning of this special day. They both smiled sheepishly. They told me how much they enjoyed planning this day together.

The drive home was quiet – all of us happily soporific after that meal.

We pulled in the driveway and I realized that we forgot to turn on the front door light when we left for dinner.

David got out the key and opened the door for us. I realized we also forgot to leave on any interior lights.

Just as I started complaining about how important it is to leave on lights so that the house looks occupied, all the living room lights turned on and people popped up from behind my rearranged living room furniture yelling "SURPRISE!!!"

Nicholas jumped up and down with glee and looked to me for my reaction. David gave everyone a thumbs-up in appreciation of their timing. My mouth hung open and my hands covered my cheeks in disbelief. I was mute.

The assembled friends rushed at me and congratulated me. They celebrated their ability to actually surprise me.

Champagne was opened and poured freely. Toasts were made. Songs were sung. Stories were told. Gifts were opened.

Warmed by champagne and the smiles of those nearest and dearest to me, I realized that I'm going to like forty.

I hugged my family close.

****

And then, while in the loving arms of my family, I wake up.

Nicholas is yelling at the top of his lungs, "Mom, Dad has fed the animals – time for you to get up!"

I blink. Once. Twice. It was all a dream. A wonderful dream. Reality crashes in.

"Earth to Mom! Dad has fed the animals – time for you to get up!"

"OK, buddy" I weakly reply.

It's Saturday. My fortieth birthday. A day just like any other day.

"C'mon, Mom, I want bacon and juice and a poptart!"

"Yeah, OK, I just have to stretch first."

"Hurry up! I'm hungry!"

I throw my legs over the side of the bed and grab my flannel robe. As my feet slide into my worn slippers I notice something other than the usual clutter on my dresser. I squint. I put my glasses over my forty-year-old eyes.

It looks like a small wooden easel. Set on the easel is a wooden frame, painted blue. I can't see what is within the frame, as there is a huge red bow stuck on it.

I tie my robe, and head over toward the mystery object. I carefully peel off the bow and ribbon. I gasp.

Inside the frame is a white piece of paper on which is printed "Je t'aime" in magic marker.

I stumble back onto the bed, staring at my gift. I know it is from Nicholas because of his current fascination with French. And I recognize that neat printing.

I clutch the frame to my chest, my heart bursting.

Oh, not a day like every other day at all.

Oh, so much better than breakfast in bed, a rose petal bath, furniture rearranging, dinner, and a party.

Oh, just the best present ever.

"C'mon Mom, get up!" Nicholas bellows from downstairs.

"Yes, I'm coming. I'll be right there," as I dab my glistening eyes and attempt to compose myself.

I wonder how I can let him know, without the luxury of hugs and kisses, how much this gift means to me. It has to be a low key idea, or he'll get overstimulated.

I know.

I grab a piece of paper and a pen from the night table. I write "Je t'aime aussi."

I leave it on his dresser in his room on my way downstairs.

"OK, breakfast coming up!" I cheer.

"Don't let Dad make it – he doesn't do it properly and…"

The sound of his demands and complaints blur into the background.

This is the best birthday ever.

Ash Wednesday (First Day of Lent)

Battle Fatigue

When I was growing up, whenever I or any of my four siblings encountered stressful situations, as adolescents inevitably do, my mother's prescription was always the same: Heffapil.

The night before a big exam, my sister would get Heffapil at bedtime. The night before my brother's driver's license road test, Heffapil. When my boyfriend dumped me the day before my Junior Achievement award speech, out came the Heffapil. Whenever the hurdles of life got to be too much, Heffapil was there.

And the script was always the same.

After hearing our dilemma, Mom would whisper in her soothing Dutch accent, "You know, I think you need Heffapil."

And then she would disappear into her bedroom, close the door, and emerge moments later with one hand closed. Like a dealer, she would look around to make sure my father wasn't in the room. That's when she would pass the stuff. She would grasp the recipient's hand, open the fingers, place the dose of Heffapil firmly into the flat palm of the recipient's hand, close the recipient's fingers around it, murmur "Take it at bedtime" and dart down the hall.

That night, we would fall into sleep easily and deeply, and awake in the morning ready to face the challenges that confronted us.

It wasn't until my late twenties that I learned that Heffapil wasn't the actual pharmaceutical name. No. It wasn't Heffapil. It was half a pill.

What the pills were, where they came from, why she had them, where she kept them, I never learned.

She was a medical secretary, so maybe her boss prescribed them after she told him of a particular dilemma she was having. Maybe they were pharmaceutical samples that she stashed in her purse when the salesman left the office. I'll never know.

But I do know that I could use a little Heffapil right about now. What a day.

It started with a jolt. The bedside radio is the first contact of the day with the outside world. I am rubbing the sleep from my eyes; David is already up to feed the pets. The morning news at the top of the hour is winding down, but they do a recap. The lead story is of a single parent in Montreal who drowned her teenage autistic son in the bathtub. I bolt straight up in bed. No further details are given.

"Nicholas, are you awake?" I instinctively call.

"You didn't mean to scare me!" is his response.

My posture softens a bit, and I reply, "No I didn't mean to scare you. I was just wondering if you were OK."

"Yeah."

I get up and throw on my robe, and head to the kitchen to turn on the television, anxious to catch some details about the story. A commercial. I begin to make Nicholas' usual breakfast of four strips of bacon, a poptart, cranberry juice, and two fish oil supplements.

Uh, oh. Out of poptarts. There will be hell to pay.

Just as the commercial is over, and the news programming is returning, David turns on the can opener to open the dog food. I have to leave the room. I hate the smell of pet food, particularly in the morning. Rats. Right now I wish we had a television in the dining room.

The pets are fed, and I return to the kitchen and my tasks. The television news is still on. But the segment is about falling stock markets.

I set the table with Nicholas' favourite placemat and napkin, and call him to the table.

"No, can I wait until the bonus round of Wheel of Fortune is finished on the computer?"

I look at the clock. The bus will be here in twenty-five minutes. The morning dance begins...

"Well, if you play it quickly, OK."

"No, I don't want to do it quickly. Can I do it slow or will that take too long? Can I do it just right?"

I look at the clock. Eighteen minutes.

"Well, I have to tell you something's different about your breakfast this morning."

He comes rushing into the room.

"We have no more poptarts. I'm sorry. I'll go write it on the grocery list right now."

"Get some today!" he orders.

I write down poptarts on the list on the fridge, and reach over and turn up the volume on the small counter television. Nope. Latest fall fashions.

From the family room: "I don't want my breakfast! There's no poptart!"

In no mood to argue, I instruct him to bring his plate into the kitchen, then go upstairs to the bathroom, and then get dressed.

He'll be a bear at school this morning with no food in his stomach.

As he's stomping up the stairs I once again turn up the volume on the television. Nope. Weather. Nicholas races down the stairs, upset.

"Did he say five degrees? He meant seven degrees – I don't like the number five!" Before I address this anxiety, comes another.

"Did he say the word new – he meant old, he meant old – I don't like the word new." His hands are flapping and tears are coming to his eyes.

"No, Nicholas, he said knew. K-N-E-W, not N-E-W. You can stay calm, and go back upstairs." He turns to go, then turns back to me.

"What am I supposed to be concentrating on? I have trouble following directions."

"You are going to first go pee, then second, go to your room to get dressed, then third, I'll come up and help you brush your teeth."

I look at the clock. Ten minutes till bus arrival.

Back to the television. They announce that they have an interview with the lawyer of the woman who drowned her autistic son coming up right after the break.

I start making his lunch. I'm way behind this morning. I glance at the clock and double my speed. Rice crackers. Celery. Chicken wings from last night's dinner. Homemade spelt flour chocolate chip cookies. Organic fruit gummy bears. Vanilla milkshake. Done. And all during the commercial break!

I hear the toilet flush. I hear the final stages of his bathroom ritual.

In the past, when we have inquired about the odd sounds that we hear coming out of the bathroom, he has told us that he pretends the toilet is a photocopying machine, and that he has to put his photocopy card into the machine, lift the lid, and photocopy. From listening outside the door ('cause there's no way he'll let us in while he's in there) we can hear the sound of him urinating while he is making a pretty credible imitation of the sound a photocopy machine makes.

Well, although odd, it is imaginative. Right?

So, the toilet flushes, just as the news resumes. I turn up the volume. And just like a well-timed joke, he calls to me, "Jennifer, can I interrupt you or do you have to listen to that important part?"

I guess I made the mistake of hesitating for a fraction of a second.

"Earth to Mom, may I have your attention or do you have many things you have to do?" He's getting agitated.

"Nicholas, can you ask your father, please?"

David is making our tea.

"No, No, I don't want to talk to David, I want to talk to you! I need you!!!!"

I turn off the television and head upstairs. I give up. There's just no point in trying to learn anything about this tragedy until after he's on the bus.

I arrive at the top of the stairs, and he grills me with the usual round of questions that I hear each and every morning. "Am I going to wear my spring shoes or my winter boots today? Am I going to wear my cap or my winter hat today? Am I going to wear my Aunt Cathy sweater and my windbreaker or my winter coat today?"

And as always, I get him to look out the window and see what kind of a day it is, and choose the most appropriate outerwear.

"But first, you need to decide what to wear under your coat, yes?"

I shoot a glance at the clock. Three minutes until soft-hearted Brian the bus driver arrives at the end of our driveway to take our special boy off to school. I hate to keep him waiting.

There's no way that Nicholas is going to make decisions about what to wear and get about the business of putting it on in three minutes. Executive decision. No independence training this morning. I'm taking charge.

I open the top drawer of his dresser and toss a pair of underwear and an undershirt onto the bed. Socks. Second drawer. Pants. Shirt. Belt.

Pull off his pajama top. Bottom. Seat him on the bed. Underwear on. Socks. Pants. Shirt. Belt.

"On Tuesday, September 17th when I was six, remember who came to visit?"

"No, I don't think I do. Remember, I don't remember things as well as you do."

"Yes, you do! Yes you do! Tuesday, September 17th!!!"

"Give me a hint." I pull up his pants and zip up the fly.

"Um. Mr. Colwell. He came to get a cheque."

"Oh right." Socks on. "Well maybe, instead of asking me to see if I know the answer, you could just tell me what you remember, and then we'll both be more calm."

Before he can argue, I walk to the bathroom to get his toothbrush. On the way, I call down to David, "Can you write a note in his communication book to school that he didn't eat any breakfast this morning and that they might want to snack him a little earlier than usual?"

"Gotcha!"

Electric toothbrush. Paste.

"Don't brush too hard, or do you have to brush hard? I want you to brush just right!"

Run water. Nicholas covers his ears.

Open mouth. Brush. Spit. Rinse. Spit.

Hands. Wash. Face.

"I won't get soap in my eyes. Don't touch my nose. That's too hard!" he swats my hands away.

Rinse. Dry.

Grab hand. Walk not run downstairs.

He does his usual game show in his mind routine, as he does every morning as we hit the second step from the top on the stairs. Today it's the introductions on Wheel of Fortune. He plays all the parts.

"We have with us today John Dartt. What do you do, John? Well, I'm an actor at Neptune Theatre in Halifax and I'm bald. Yes, hello, my name is Joan Ferguson, and I'm a teacher at Prospect Road Elementary School. I can give John Levesque some of my hair. And finally we have Richard Dawson. I'm the host of Family Feud. I like it when people win the big money. I don't like it when they get the answer wrong." He makes the sound of a buzzer. All the while David and I have been outfitting him in his coat and boots and hat.

I see the bus pull up.

"Nicholas?"

"Wait, I have to mute." He makes a sound that indicates he is muting the game show in his head. "Yes, Mommy?"

"I want you to remember to have great behaviour at school today, OK?"

"Or else will I have to go to a different school and you guarantee I won't like it?"

"Because it's the rule of the school. They like to have children that behave – they don't like to have children that don't behave. Understand?"

"I understand."

"OK. Love you. Have a great day."

"Yeah."

He is walking out the door with David, clearly having un-muted the game show in his head. The two of them walk down to the end of the driveway, Nicholas making the sound of the Wheel of Fortune wheel spinning, and then a buzzer sound as apparently John Dartt or Ms. Ferguson or Richard Dawson hit the bankrupt space on the wheel.

I watch him board the bus, feeling like I've just completed the qualifying trials for the Mom Olympics.

Every morning is the same. The same breakfast, answering the same questions, following the same rituals, defusing the same anxieties. Morning after morning.

What I wouldn't give for a little spontaneity.

I return to the kitchen and the cup of tea David has made for me. Cold now. Turn on the television. The news program is over. I scan the stations looking for another Canadian news show. Nothing.

I instruct David to keep his eye and ear on the radio and TV to catch something while I'm in the shower.

The shower is my sanctuary. My haven. It's private. Remote. Warm. Soothing. Rejuvenating. Some days I wish I could spend hours in the shower. But not today. There is no hot water.

"DAVID!"

He runs upstairs, rushing into the bathroom like he expected to find me flat on my back on the slippery floor, writhing in pain.

"There's no hot water!"

I throw my robe over me and stomp downstairs. I guess I'll have to work a little first, then take my shower.

I open my briefcase and take out some papers. I'll get this marking done, shower, plan Wednesday's class, stack wood, meet Nic's bus, do homework with him, attend the school team meeting, make dinner, and go to the Autism Support Group meeting tonight.

But in order for any of this to happen, the hot water has got to come back.

I turn on the radio in my study, hoping something about the event in Montreal comes on. The event in Montreal. I can't even say it. The woman who drowned her autistic son. A shiver runs down my spine.

As I open my binder and remove students' papers, I wonder how such a thing could happen. How can a parent be driven to this? Where were her support systems?

I place the papers in a pile and take the top one and place it in front of me on the desk. I read the student's name.

The phone rings. It's the school. We forgot to pack Nicholas' headphones in his school bag this morning and he is quite anxious in the classroom without them. Could we drive them over? Sure.

"David, are you dressed? Can you drive Nic's headphones over to the school?"

"Jennifer, I'm in the middle of replacing the hot water fuse."

I sigh. "Yeah, OK, carry on."

I brush my oily hair and tie it back. Look in the mirror. Not a stitch of makeup. Hope I don't scare them. Grab his headphones from the couch. Grab keys. Out the door.

I return to find David in the shower. Good. Hot water. I call through the steam, "Do you think your faculty meeting will be done in time for you to be home in time for me to get to Nicholas' school for the three-fifteen meeting?"

A garbled "Yes."

Heat up my tea, grab a banana, head back to my papers.

I work for a couple of hours, half of my mind on my marking, the other half listening for news of the Montreal woman and her son. Nothing.

And the papers I'm marking are disappointing too.

David's gone now. I can shower. Well, no, maybe it makes more sense to stack wood and then shower.

Vanna the dog and I go outside into the cold spring air and are confronted by five cords of wood in an overwhelming heap in the middle of the driveway.

I get the wheelbarrow and my gloves, determined to engage happily in some therapeutic physical activity to clear my mind. But all I can think about is the woman in Montreal.

I know that even if I don't manage to hear anything more about it on the news today, someone at tonight's meeting will know the details.

I toss a load of wood into the wheelbarrow.

Was it burnout? Being a single parent having to care for and nurture an autistic child alone?

I stack the load by the basement door.

I shudder. Raising my autistic son is certainly the greatest challenge of my life. I couldn't imagine having to do it alone.

Another load into the wheelbarrow.

Where were her family and friends? Respite? Community services?

Another load stacked. And another. And another. I lose track of time and the number of loads of wood.

My heart aches. For the boy. For the woman. For us all.

OK. That's about a cord stacked. Just as I go to get another load from the driveway, I hear a cracking thump. I look back. The entire stack has fallen over. I curse.

Just then Nicholas' bus pulls up. What, is it that time already? I'm way behind. I haven't even prepared his after school agenda. And now I have to restack this wood? No. It will have to wait.

Vanna and I walk to the bus. Brian opens the door and Vanna runs on board to get her daily treat of two dog biscuits. Brian gets them from a caddy below his dash, which is filled with the various favourite brands of all the dogs on his route. He holds out his hand for her.

While Vanna loves this ritual, its Norman Rockwell cuteness is lost on Nicholas. "Put her back on her tether," he begs, not able to cope with her puppy enthusiasm and her wanting to lick his face.

I assure him I will, and we leave the bus, me reminding him to say goodbye to Brian. Not just say it but wave as well.

We walk to the backyard and put Vanna on her tether, leaving her to devour her treats.

"How was school today, buddy?"

"Fine."

"What did you do today?" I know this is too vague for him. "What did you do in math today?" I rephrase.

"I'm not sure."

"How was your behaviour today?"

"So-so."

We walk past the fallen wood. He doesn't even notice.

Once inside, I tell him that he can do what he wants for an hour, and then we will do homework. Does he want to play a game of Guess Who with me?

No. He heads off to the computer. Shuts the door. I'm disappointed, but he is entitled to his decompression time.

Comes out to ask me how many seconds are in twenty-three minutes. And without waiting for an answer, tells me the answer is thirteen hundred and eighty. How does he do that?!

I take his school bag into the kitchen and open it. I reach for the communication book. Open it to today's date, and read with a combination of frustration and dismay that he had twelve time outs today. Mostly this morning. I know that this will have to be addressed at this afternoon's meeting. I take note of what homework he has been assigned, and empty his lunch containers. Didn't eat much lunch either. Could be a rough afternoon. Great.

While he is playing computer games, I organize this after-noon's agenda. Let's see. What shall we work on this afternoon? His school work first. Math. Then study for tomorrow's spelling test. Then reading comprehension. Then our own stuff: Shoelace tying, drawing, basketball practice.

I write out the agenda for him, then set about gathering the materials we'll need: the step-by-step written instruction manual I made for shoelace tying; one of my old sneakers with an orange lace in the left side and a green lace on the right side to help him visually; the book with step-by-step instructions on how to draw simple animals; set up the basketball net and the ball in the driveway.

I knock on the closed study door and enter.

"I want privacy! I want privacy! Don't disturb me! Or do you need to be here?" he screams. I remind him to keep his voice volume low, and that I came in to ask him if he wanted a snack of peanut butter and crackers in the family room.

"No!" he screams, "Peanut butter is too soft!"

"Volume," I remind him. "Then how about peanuts and raisins mixed together in a bowl."

"Yes, but later, when I've finished the bonus round."

I can live with that. I take the opportunity to remind him that I have a meeting at the school this afternoon, and that when I get back, we will do homework.

"Take Club Road when you go to the school. Don't go the other way! I don't like it when you go the other way!"

I assure him I will go the Club Road way.

I go fix his snack, and place it near his favourite spot in the family room.

I look at the clock. Three o'clock! I have to be at the school in fifteen minutes. I haven't showered yet today! I'm wearing my overalls and covered with wood chips! And where is David??!!!

OK. Prioritize. Shower is out of the question. I cringe. Change of clothes. A little lipstick. Definitely a ballcap over the greasy hair. I wonder if they'll be on to me? Of course they will.

Where is David???!!!!

It's three-ten. I grab my bag and stuff a notebook and pen into it.

I halt my pacing to knock on the study door again.

"Don't scare me!"

"I'm sorry, Nicholas, but I want you to know that your snack is ready in the family room, and as soon as Dad arrives, I'm going to the meeting, and yes, I will take Club Road."

The clock on the study wall reads three-fifteen.

"Close the door all the way!" Nicholas booms. I do.

Where's David!!!???

Just as I'm starting to fume, he pulls up. He opens his mouth to apologize, but I've already pulled him out of the car and thrown my bag and myself into it. I throw it into gear, and take off, careful to turn left at the end of the driveway onto Club Road, because I know Nicholas will be standing in the living room window watching to make sure I do.

I arrive at the school and walk into the resource teacher's room, spouting apologies for being late.

I take a seat on a child-size chair at a small round table, around which are seated Nicholas' classroom teacher, the principal, the resource teacher, his speech and language pathologist, his classroom educational assistant, and the school psychologist. All very supportive. All sitting on child-size chairs too.

I'm nervous, wanting, and yet not wanting, to know how Nicholas has been faring at school so far this year.

The resource teacher leads the discussion, and the first topic is concern about his behaviour. I knew it. I stiffen.

He is having a lot of time outs. We refer to the list of things for which he gets timed out. They are categorized into: Verbal Behaviours, Non-Compliance Behaviours, and Aggressive Behaviours. The aggressive behaviour is on the rise, and there is great concern about it escalating any further.

They ask for my input on working toward reducing the number of time outs, and eliminating the aggressive behaviour.

I understand that Nicholas is the first autistic child they have had attend the school, and they are cutting their teeth on him.

I explain, once again, that time outs may not be the best behavioural remedy for Nicholas at school, as we have been dealing with these same problems for a few years now. And once we seem to solve one behavioural problem, another pops up. I remind them that he will deliberately do things to get into time out, particularly if something is being done in the classroom that is challenging for him. He would much prefer to sit on his beanbag in the hallway than tackle a tough math problem. Yes, at home time out is more effective, partly because the atmosphere is not as stressful as at school, and partly because he enjoys doing things at home and doesn't like to be separated from them.

The discussion continues for an hour. We talk about environmental factors in the classroom, reinforcers, balancing his time spent in the classroom versus quiet learning time in the resource room, presentation of the work, giving appropriate breaks. In the end we agree to call in the autism behavioural specialist on the school board. I'm warned that she is in high demand and may not be able to visit as soon as we'd like. But we have to wait, as David and I have brought in just about every private psychologist in the city, and nothing they have tried has been effective.

The other items on the meeting agenda will also have to wait until the next team meeting.

I smile and say thank-yous and goodbyes and run to the car. Four-thirty. I fasten my seatbelt and drive faster than I should out of the school yard.

I realize that my jaw is clenched and my knuckles are white around the steering wheel. My head is pounding. I turn up the music very loud. I pull the car off the side of the road. I scream at the top of my lungs.

Some days, like today, I don't want to be his teacher, his advocate, his behavioural specialist, his developmental trainer.

Some days I just want to be his mother.

I consider dropping by the community pharmacy and begging for a couple of Heffapils. Surely they would know what Heffapil is, and would have a few just lying around in a drawer somewhere.

I return to the road and make for Club Road. Moments later I'm walking through the front door. Throat sore. Head still pounding. I take two deep breaths.

"Hi guys!" I chirp.

Nicholas comes running to the door.

"It's past four-thirty! Homework time!" His hands flapping in agitation.

"How about 'Hi Mom' first?"

David comes out of the family room and asks how the meeting went. I inhale and roll my eyes upwards. "Our kid is a monster," I whisper.

Nicholas pulls at my arm. "Homework time! I don't want to miss the start of Gilligan's Island!"

I am dragged into the family room, kicking off my shoes and unzipping my coat as I go.

David follows and asks, "What happened to the wood?" I inhale and smile, and open my mouth to speak.

"Mom, I need your attention, I need your attention now!"

"Nicholas, please don't interrupt – I'm having a conversation with Dad."

"No, but I don't want you to say anything I don't like!"

I go to the kitchen and fetch his headphones out of his school bag and put them over my ears. A visual cue for him not to interrupt. It doesn't work today.

"Jennifer, I need to talk to you or do you have many things to say?"

I point up the stairs to his room.

"What am I being timed out for?"

"Interrupting. Now get going."

I set the timer for five minutes, take off the headphones, and return to the family room to have a five-minute conversation with my husband.

We discuss the events of the meeting, his faculty meeting, the wood fiasco, what Nicholas ate while I was gone, any calls and messages for each other.

The timer dings. Nicholas comes out of his room.

"Is interrupting a verbal behaviour, a non-compliance behaviour, or an aggressive behaviour?"

I start to tell him that we don't talk about time outs when they are over, when I notice his wet pants.

"Nicholas, what happened?" I ask.

"I had an accident when I was in time out."

This is not the first time this has happened.

"Remember, you can come out of time out to go to the bathroom if you need to, right?"

He nods. I fluctuate between wondering if he does this deliberately to pay me back for timing him out, and wondering if he was squirming in his time-out chair trying to hold it in and I'm the most insensitive mother in the world for putting him through that.

"OK. Change your clothes, and then we'll do homework."

When he returns to the family room with his clean pants and shirt on backwards, I wonder whether to let it go or address it. I decide to let it go, knowing that we are about to launch into stress-laden homework territory.

He reads the homework itinerary, and we set to work. I take my usual seat opposite him at the table because he can't tolerate me on the same side as him. He claims I'm too close.

First math. His first time out is for throwing his pencil. His second time out is for breaking his pencil. Homework is going to take a particularly long time this afternoon.

An hour and a half later, we are done. Exhausted, drained, like boxers in our respective corners.

Some days the constant non-compliance makes me want to throw up my hands and give up.

I leave him in David's hands and go to the backyard to spend some time with the dog to get a much-needed dose of affection and appreciation.

As the dog and I run and laugh, I wonder how the woman in Montreal is doing right now.

From inside the house I hear Nicholas yelling, "I hate you, I don't like you anymore, I'm hurting your feelings! I'm dying – my feelings are broken – the world fell apart!" I sigh.

I see the clock upon my return into the house. How did it get to be so late? My support group meeting starts in an hour and a half, and I haven't even thought about dinner yet!

"Where is Nic?" I ask as David sits reading the paper.

"In time out."

I look to the time-out timer and notice that it has been set way past the standard five minutes.

David looks up from his newspaper and flashes a mischievous smile.

"Uh, OK, spaghetti for dinner. David, I'll rip the lettuce. You chop the veggies. I'll make sauce. Go!"

We rush around the kitchen, managing something resembling a conversation between the fetching, chopping, and stirring.

The time-out timer dings. I hear Nicholas upstairs, "I prefer to be in there another thirty seconds."

"Fine."

David and I share a look of relief. Thirty more seconds of uninterrupted conversation…

The dinner is prepped and simmering. When Nicholas comes out of his room, he asks what is for dinner and what time it will be ready. He is not happy with either answer.

He screams, "I don't want dinner, I want to go on my plane, I'm sick!" He bangs his head on the dining room floor. I send him to his room, ignoring his questions about what category of behaviour head-banging falls under.

He hates it when he is ignored. That's why it's useful.

His voice pitches up, and he gets increasingly agitated, repeating the question over and over, crying. I climb the stairs, take him by the hand, put him in his room, and close the door. I hear things smashing as I descend the stairs and set the timer not for five, but for ten minutes.

"David, see if you can find something on the news about the woman in Montreal while Nic is in time out."

I stir the sauce and make Nicholas' salad just the way he likes it: crunchy and full of bold flavours. I place it on the table, so that he can start on that while the pasta cooks.

The time-out timer dings just as the stove-top timer dings, signaling that the spaghetti is finished.

Nicholas comes out of his room, his pants wet again.

I tell David to start dinner. I tell Nicholas I am running him a bath.

"No, it's not bath night – No bath!!!"

I ignore his protests and take him into the bathroom.

He gives me a lot of grief about it, but I manage to bathe him and get him into his pajamas. I look at my arm to where he pinched me while I washed his face. That'll be a nice bruise tomorrow.

I suddenly remember that the woman in Montreal drowned her son in the bathtub.

We sit down to dinner in the family room. Nicholas finds his beloved Wheel of Fortune on television, and digs in to his salad and spaghetti with his hands. I get his attention and hold up my fork as a reminder.

After Wheel of Fortune comes Whose Line Is It Anyway? – the American version. Nicholas lives for the end of that show. He loves it when they end the show with a 'hoe-down'; he's devastated when they don't. As fate would have it, tonight they don't.

"I want to turn that off. I never want to watch Whose Line ever again," he rants. "I hate it when they don't do a hoe-down. I hate Drew Carey. I want to hurt his feelings! How will he feel about that?"

Another family dinner.

I am eerily calm. "Now go brush your teeth, and get on your plane. I will bring up your water and pills."

He opens his mouth to protest.

I walk over to him and take him by the hand and take him upstairs and put him in the bathroom. He cries and screams.

I come downstairs, pour him a fresh glass of water, take two fish oil pills from the cabinet and return upstairs.

I open the bathroom door and find him with his hand-held Wheel of Fortune game. I remove it from his hands amidst a gush of tears, brush his teeth, turn off the bathroom lights and escort him to his bed. He climbs on his "plane" as he calls it. Tonight I wish it was a plane.

He takes his pills. Lights out. No stories tonight. Blow a kiss and walk away. Downstairs.

I sit down at the table and raise the fork to my mouth.

Nicholas is yelling, "I'm going to stay awake all night!"

I twirl my spaghetti around my fork.

I surprise myself by saying, "I don't think I'm going to the support meeting tonight."

David gives me a well-maybe-you-should look.

"Nope. I'm autism-ed out. If I hear another word about autism today, I'll scream. Nope. I'm going to put on my pajamas and read a book, and maybe lie on the couch with my head in your lap for a little while. Oh, did you manage to find anything about the Montreal woman on the news?"

"Not a thing."

I take my empty plate into the kitchen and pour myself a glass of wine. I grab my book, and before heading upstairs, I reach into Nicholas' school bag and find his headphones. I head up the stairs.

Nicholas is still crying and screaming.

I change out of my clothes, sink into my favourite chair, take a sip of wine, and place my son's headphones over my ears.

I let out a long sigh. It's no Heffapil, but it will do.

I leaf through the pages to where I left off reading.

My eyes open wide.

Oh no! I forgot to buy poptarts today! There will be hell to pay tomorrow morning. Oh no!

Another Heffapil day coming up?

Easter Sunday

Acceptance

Nicholas' fascination with God, and his attempt to make concrete the abstract concept of heaven, began after our traditional Easter egg hunt on Easter morning.

The previous evening he had written his traditional note to the Easter Bunny asking for the traditional haul of chocolate eggs and the traditional big chocolate bunny. In keeping with tradition, he placed the note outside the front door, along with the few traditional carrots.

Easter morning he woke us at the crack of dawn. This was particularly onerous for me as I had been at the theatre late the night before and had a matinee performance in just a few short hours.

But Nicholas had no compassion for my complaints, pulling me out of bed by my arm. Needless to say, he loves tradition. And chocolate.

Of course, Easter morning was traditionally rainy. Pouring, in fact. Great.

After a quick traditional breakfast of hot cross buns, we donned our slickers and boots, grabbed the traditional red basket for collecting the goodies, and headed out into the garden to find what the Easter Bunny had left for Nicholas.

He was excited, yet nervous. "Some squirrels might knock me over," he worried.

After we assured him that we would keep squirrels away, and reminded him that there was probably a chocolate egg behind that big grey rock over there, he clutched his basket and started the hunt.

Two dozen foil-wrapped mini eggs later, and chilled to the bone, we figured we had found all the treasure there was to be found in the garden, and suggested to Nicholas that we return to the house just in case the Easter Bunny had managed to let himself in and leave some extra treats hidden inside the house.

As we removed our rain gear, I noticed Nicholas' bangs had got wet.

"Your hair got a little wet," I commented.

Without pausing, he replied, "Yeah, just like when I was a baby in church and God wanted my head to be damp."

I froze.

I shot a look to David. He was frozen too.

We didn't breathe. We didn't move. In those few frozen moments only our eyes spoke.

Our eyes asked one another to what event Nicholas was referring. Are you thinking what I'm thinking? Our eyebrows arched: could he have heard about it at church? No, we in fact hadn't been to church since then. Our eyes dipped in shame. Then they sparkled with another possibility: could he have overheard us talking about it? No, we were both sure we had never discussed it. Our eyes lowered. My eyes looked up to David's. Maybe he saw a picture of the event. No, the only photographs taken were at the house afterwards, and the only written record was a certificate glued into a photo album which was tucked away in the basement. Our eyes met straight on with cold numbness. All four of our eyes agreed on the only, albeit astounding, conclusion: he remembered it!

Yes, what he had just referred to happened when he was only ten months old. He was talking about his own baptism!

David and I finally exhaled enough to ask the question.

I volunteered, posing it delicately and with great reverence, as one would when addressing a superhero with extraordinary powers.

"Nicholas, do you remember being in church?"

Popping a chocolate egg into his mouth, "Yes. I giggled when my hair got damp."

I was sure my sharp inhalation was audible.

There was my proof. He HAD giggled when the minister sprinkled water on his head. I remember turning to David and commenting that most babies would cry, but our son giggled. It would turn out to be his first of many incidents of inappropriate giggling.

Oh. My. God.

Our little superhero was anxious for us to accompany him upstairs to scour window ledges and room corners for more eggs. Not for a moment did he wonder how the Easter Bunny might have entered our house in the middle of the night. Nor for a moment did he consider the possibility that the Easter Bunny might not be real.

We searched upstairs, and in fact the Easter Bunny had managed to find a few more hiding spots in various rooms up there, and the hunt concluded with the discovery of the solid chocolate bunny at the foot of his bed. True to tradition, he asked if he could eat the ears.

Out of nowhere, with the Van Gogh-ed bunny in one hand, his other hand counting all the eggs in his basket, and his face covered in chocolate, he asked the question: a question that we weren't sure we would ever have to field.

"What's God's last name?"

Just as we were ecstatic to hear him tell his first lie at age six, we were thrilled to hear this question emerge from his chocolate lips.

My eyes urged David's eyes to take this one on.

"I don't think God has a last name," David offered.

"Yes, he does!" Nicholas insisted, "Everyone has a last name! Mom said so on Monday October 23rd!"

How could anyone argue with that defense?

It was still in David's court. Being the quick and nimble thinker that he is, he came up with the answer. "Almighty," he said confidently.

My eyes shot David's eyes a visual high five. More like a wink.

"God Almighty." Nic tasted the name in his chocolate-lined mouth. "I'll have to look that up in the phone book under 'A' and give him a call."

In my head, I immediately began spinning the story that I would have to make up to deal with the inevitable situation which is bound to arise when he tries to find God's phone number in the phone directory. It would involve something about God having an unlisted number or something.

He then wanted to know God's middle name, the names of his family members, and if God learned his job at Heaven University.

David and I sat down with him and told him a simple version of the story of Jesus, and that Jesus was God's son and that he died and went to live with his father in Heaven.

"How did he die? Did he have cancer or a heart attack, or both? Or did he die because he was old, or did he work too hard? Did he have cancer like Uncle Robert from smoking too many cigarettes? Did his body want cigarettes or did the cigarettes just fall out of the package into his mouth?"

We tried to explain that he died because some men didn't like him and were mean to him.

"Did they bully him?" he asked.

"Yes, I guess they did bully him." I answered. That was a fair interpretation we thought.

I looked at the clock. I had to get moving.

Once convinced that he had asked all the questions he wanted to at the moment, we decided his chocolate rations for the next few days, and I went into the shower to get ready for work. On matinee days I like to be at the theatre for noon so as not to be rushed with hair and makeup and my own traditional preparatory rituals before show time.

While in the shower, I wondered if he was asking David more questions right now, being a 'dog with a bone' once he got an idea into his head. I was sorry I was missing them.

Then I turned my thoughts to the show.

The irony is not lost on me that the areas of myself that I use in my performing are exactly the areas that challenge Nicholas.

In my work, I explore and communicate emotion. Nicholas has difficulty understanding emotions beyond the most basic level.

I am a student of human behaviour. Nicholas has difficulty interpreting human actions.

I rely on abstract images when creating a character. Nicholas lives in a very concrete world.

I employ a great deal of instinct and intuition to lead me in my work. Nicholas has to be taught explicitly what we intuit.

I explore the subtleties and nuances of the human condition. Nicholas insists on black and white.

I investigate the dynamics of human relationships. Human relationships baffle Nicholas.

I thought about the play itself, an exciting new Canadian comedy called *Kilt*, written by Jonathan Wilson. It is the story of a young Canadian gay man and his relationship, or rather, non-relationship with his very Scottish mother, who refuses to recognize his homosexuality. During the course of the play, however, they come to accept each other, and agree to forge a relationship out of the ruins.

I play the mother.

The mother's emotional journey in the play is what interested me in the role. At the beginning of the play, she sees only her son's deviance and his unwillingness to meet her high standards. She doesn't see that her rigidity costs her his love.

The last moment of the play is of mother and son tentatively, awkwardly, embracing.

Hilarious as the play is – I mean, imagine a conservative uptight mother arriving at the bar where she is told her son works, only to discover that it is in fact a strip club, and she arrives just in time to see her son in the middle of his act, wearing his grandfather's traditional, sacred kilt! – but it is in the final touching reconciliation that the play resonates and its characters come together.

I get great satisfaction hearing the sniffles in the audience when I as the mother hug my son at the end of the play. And no one in the audience or on stage knows that in my mind, I am actually imagining that after years of yearning but being prohibited because of his sensitivity to touch, I am finally, at long last, invited to hug my real-life son, my Nicholas, at that moment. Tears of joy and wonder spring out of me at every performance.

Acceptance. She finally comes to accept her son for what he is, not what she hoped he would be.

Art imitating life.

Anyway, the reviews were good. And that gives me hope for the real-life part.

Once clean and dressed and philosophized out, I returned downstairs to pack a light lunch to take with me to the theatre. Nicholas was in the family room with a container of plastic food.

"What are you doing?" I asked.

"Having a picnic with God and Mary and Jesus Almighty and Thomas Edison and Anthony Newley and Ricky Nelson and Uncle Robert and Oma and Opa and Emily the dog and Maude the cat. Apparently Jesus' favourite food is pickles."

A piece of paper taped to the wall beside where he was playing caught my eye. On it was written: City of Heaven.

I asked if I could play too.

"No, Jennifer, we would prefer to be alone."

Much as I wanted to join in, I decided to respect, accept, his decision.

I went into the kitchen and put together my bag lunch. A small serving of pasta and chicken, celery, and an apple.

Through the doorway I saw Nicholas put his hands together, mutter something about "thank you," then stand up and bow. He was saying a prayer! And I knew immediately, instinctively, what the bow was about. I quietly entered the family room and apologized for interrupting. I reminded him that bowing your head to pray meant that you let your head fall a little forward – I demonstrated – it did not mean that you bowed at the end of the prayer. Too cute.

"Will the actors bow at the end of the play today?"

I told him they would.

"Will God be in the audience today?"

I told him I hoped so.

He asked what time I would be back from the theatre. I told him four-thirty.

I put my lunch into my bag, put my wet slicker on, and grabbed an umbrella. I kissed David goodbye. He wished me a good show. I told him I wasn't sure there would be a very big house on Easter Sunday. Before putting on my boots, I walked into the family room and told Nicholas I was leaving to go to the theatre.

Engrossed in his heavenly picnic, he barely glanced at me, but responded to my "See ya later alligator" with the traditional "In a while crocodile."

"Enjoy your picnic," I called to him as I walked to the front door.

Pulling on my wellingtons, I remembered the City of Heaven sign he had stuck on the wall above his play area.

I called back to him from the front door. "Nicholas, by the way, where is Heaven?"

He said matter-of-factly from the family room, "Off Quinpool Road."

"Hmmm. The home owners in that area will be happy to hear that," I said to David. "Real-estate values will skyrocket!"

David's eyes laughed.

I left to go and perform my play about acceptance.

April 28th, Our Wedding Anniversary

First Comes Love

Drum Roll

Theme Music Up

Audience Applause

Flashing Lights

Off-Camera Announcer: And now it's time for – you guessed it –

Audience shouts: *First comes love*

Then comes marriage

Then comes a bundle in a baby carriage!

Off-Camera Announcer: Or, for the families out there that were created in a different sequence: "First comes love, marriage may come later, for now here's baby in a large perambulator!"

Audience claps and laughs

Off-Camera Announcer: Welcome to your favourite game show, First Comes Love, where each of our three pre-conception souls here today plays to be matched up with one of our three sets of parents, and everyone goes home a winner! And now, here's the host of our show, the man with a nose for matchmaking; the man whose mother encourages him to play with matches; heeeere's Wink Bardo!!!

Audience Applause

Spotlight

Theme Music Up

Wink Bardo enters the spotlight, waving to the cheering audience.

Wink: Thank you Johnny. Ladies and gentlemen, here today, right before your eyes, we are going to match up babies and parents, and we hope it works out, because contestants, what you go home with today, you go home with for life. We are playing for keeps here, people!

Audience cheers and applauds

Wink: OK, let's meet our three couples, and find out a little about them. Couple Number One?

Couple#1: Yes, hello Wink. We've been waiting to get on the show for a long time, longing to get pregnant. Our names are Bert and Betty, and we live in Flint, Michigan, U.S.A. I am a sales executive for a major computer company, and Betty is a full-time homemaker. We have three children already, and are so excited about the possibility of another little one to grace our lives.

Wink: Thank you Couple Number One. Couple Number Two, tell us a little about yourselves.

Couple#2: Uh, it's so nice to meet you Wink. Inga and I live in rural Sweden, about two hundred kilometers outside Sundsvall. We are both twenty-seven years old, and in excellent health.

Wink: Isn't it infact true that Inga, you are a world class champion cross-country skier?

Couple#2: That's correct, Wink.

Wink: And what do you do when you are not swooshing past the snowy fjords?

Couple #2: We are biologists, and now we think we are ready to create and study some new life of our own! Thank you.

Wink: And last but not least, today's Couple Number Three.

Couple#3: Hello everybody. David and I, oh, my name's Jennifer, we live in Halifax, Nova Scotia, Canada, and we were married last year. David is a professor at Dalhousie University, and I'm an actor, writer, and I also teach part-time at the university at present. We would like a little one to love and nurture.

Wink: Well, we certainly have three interesting couples here with us today. Couples, if you would, please take your seats on the panel. Audience and those at home, please turn your attention to the monitors placed at the feet of each of the three couples, because it's time to say hello to today's Persons in Progress, or PIPs as we call them, the three souls waiting to be matched up with parents here today on our show. Introduce them, Johnny!

Off-Camera Announcer: Able to be with us through the miracle of satellite communications, we have with us into the studio today on these monitors our three Persons in Progress. They are not able to tell us anything about themselves as they haven't experienced this life yet, but audience, let's have a big round of applause for PIP Number One.

Audience applause

Close up on the screen on Monitor#1. The image is grainy and pulsating, with a hint of a shadow somewhere in the picture, much like an ultrasound.

Off-Camera Announcer: Welcome PIP Number Two, glad to have you with us.

Audience applause

Close up on Monitor#2. Resembles Monitor#1.

Off-Camera Announcer: and PIP Number Three, give a wave to our studio audience and to the folks at home.

Audience applause

Close up on Monitor#3. Resembles the others, but there is a ripple on the screen, indicating a wave.

Wink: Thank you Johnny. The rules of the game, as you all know are as follows:
Neither the parents nor the PIPs can see each other. The PIPs are asked a skill-testing question, and the PIP whose monitor lights up first and answers correctly earns the right to pull the lever on our cosmic-link slot machine, which has been programmed with the pictures of today's three sets of parents. PIPs win 500 points toward a Couple when their pull of the lever brings up the picture of that Couple. The slots are also loaded with pictures of fantastic prizes. But watch out for the picture of the stinky diaper! If the stinky diaper appears, you lose all your points and prizes. At the end of the game, each PIP will soon be conceived by the parents for which they have accumulated the most points!
OK, let's start the game. And remember, we're playing for keeps here, people!

Audience applause

Boost theme music. Fade theme music

Wink: PIPs, here is the first skill-testing question:

In terms of development, when are babies generally expected to first smile at their parents? Is it at five weeks of age, six months, or one year?

PIP#2 monitor lights up.

Wink: Yes, PIP#2.

PIP#2: I believe it's five weeks of age, but they would smile at six months and one year, too.

Audience applause and laughter

Wink: Well, technically, you are right PIP#2! You answered the question correctly: five weeks of age is when babies are expected to first smile. And indeed, hopefully, for the rest of their lives. PIP#2, you'll be smiling at one of these lucky Couples very soon. Your answer has earned you the right to pull the lever first on today's game.

The image on PIP#2's monitor pulses, and employing cosmic telekenesis, the lever on the giant slot machine in the studio pulls downward. First comes up the picture of Couple#3, then Couple#2, then Couple#3 again.

Wink: OK PIP#2, you've earned 500 points for Couple#2, and 1000 points towards Couple#3!
Next question: What is generally considered better for babies, breastfeeding, or bottle feeding?

PIP#1 monitor lights up.

Wink: PIP#1 lit up first this time. Pip#1?

Pip#1: I believe breastfeeding, when possible, is the best for baby.

Wink: Absolutely right, #1. Pull the lever.

The lever is pulled down. Three pictures in a row of Couple#1

Wink: Lady Luck is with you tonight it seems. You've just earned 1500 points toward Couple#1, plus a bonus prize of a $5000 college fund. Well done PIP#1!

Next question: Teething can be a difficult time for infants and parents alike. What is teething?

PIP#3 monitor lights up.

Wink: Number three?

PIP#3: I think it has to do with dental structure and formation.

Wink: We've got a smart bunch of PIPs here today on the show You're absolutely right! Give the lever a pull.

The lever is seen pulled down. Up come pictures of Couple#2, then Couple#3, then a stinky diaper.

Wink: Oh no! So early in the game to see a stinky diaper. Well #3, nothing gained, nothing lost, you remain at zero points, and we take our first commercial break. Stay tuned!

Audience applause

COMMERCIAL BREAK

Audience applause

Wink: We're back. And we're right in the thick of the game. Let's look at the scoreboard at the end of our first round. PIP#1 has 1500 points towards Couple#1, plus the college fund; PIP#2 has 500 points towards Couple#2 and 1000 points toward Couple#3; while PIP#3 has yet to score.
So. On to round two where the questions will challenge your understanding of the world you are about to enter.
Question#1: Name an endangered species.

PIP#3 monitor lights up.

Wink: #3?

PIP#3: The Bengal tiger.

Wink: Well done. That earns you the chance to score by pulling the lever.

The lever is pulled. Up come the faces of Couple#1, Couple#2, and Couple#3.

Wink: Well, you've scored five hundred points towards each of the couples here today. This could be an interesting game.

On to the next question, and let me preface it by telling you that this question has no right or wrong answer, but rather, our judges will decide if your response is worthy of a lever pull. Here's the question. When you reach young adulthood, what steps will you take to reduce green house gases?

PIP#2 monitor lights up

Wink: Yes, PIP#2?

PIP#2: I will take steps to the recycling depot. I hope the recycling depot will be a minimum of three and a maximum of two hundred steps from my house.

Wink: (looking at the judges) Mmmm…No, I'm sorry, while an interesting take on the question, and a fun example of word play, that answer is not considered sufficient. Sorry, PIP#2, your response does not earn you a pull. PIP#1or #3?

PIP#1 monitor lights up.

Wink: PIP#1, what is your answer?

PIP#1: Well, if an alternative, more efficient non-fossil fuel burning mode of transportation, something different from the automobile, has not yet been invented and in use by the time I reach age sixteen, I would devote my adult life to inventing and designing such a vehicle.

Audience applause

Wink: Yes, the judges like that answer a great deal, so PIP#1, pull that lever!

The lever is pulled. Pictures of Couple#1, then Couple#2, then Couple#1.

Wink: Looks like strong matching potential with Couple #1, and if you manage to hang on to that college tuition prize, Couple#1 may very well be raising an environmental engineer.

Wink: And now for the last question of this round. It is estimated that in the year 2025, world poverty will be abolished. True or False?

PIP #3monitor lights up

Wink: Yes, #3.

PIP#3: False. In fact Wink, if current global policies continue, world poverty will have doubled by that time.

Wink: Well done indeed PIP#3, you've clearly done your homework on the subject. Go ahead and pull the lever.

The lever is pulled. Pictures of Couple #2, then Couple#3, then Couple#2.

Wink: OK. Let's take a quick look at the score board to see where each couple and PIP stand before we take another commercial break. As we can see, each PIP has scored points toward each of the couples. PIP#1 has scored biggest with Couple#1, earning 2500 points toward them, and of course standing to win that college fund. PIP#2 has been a little slower to score but has managed an impressive 1000 points toward Couple#3. PIP#3, after this round, stands to have the best chance with 1500 points toward Couple#2. We see matching patterns emerging, but might everything be upset in our final round? Stay tuned.

Audience applause

COMMERCIAL BREAK

Audience applause

Wink: Welcome back! We're into the last round here on First
    Comes Love. The questions in this round are framed in such a
    way as to test the PIPs' quick thinking skills in the category of
    Noble Occupations. I'm going to list three things, and PIPs,
    light up your monitor when you think you know the occupa-
    tion indicated by those three items. For example, I might say:
    scalpel, surgery gown, healthy bank account, and you might
    guess surgeon. OK? Let's start with the first list of three items:
    Whisk, white hat, batter

PIP#2 monitor lights up.

Wink: Yes, #2?

PIP#2: A baseball umpire?

Audience laughter

Wink: Yes, I can now see how you came up with that, however,
    that's not the answer we're looking for here today. Anyone else
    care to guess?

PIP#1 monitor lights up.

Wink: PIP#1.

PIP#1: A chef.

Wink looks to the judges

Wink: Can you be more specific please?

PIP#1: A Pastry Chef!

Wink: Yes, that's the occupation we were looking for. Well done
    PIP#1 Pull that lever!

The lever is pulled. Pictures of Couple#1, Couple#1, and a stinky diaper.

Audience moans.

Wink: Oh no, just when it looked like you were meant to be matched up with Couple#1, the stinky diaper has wiped out all your points and, unfortunately, your college fund as well, so PIP#1, you return to zero, and our game is taking an interesting twist.
On to the next list:
Business suit, power, stock options

Pip#2 monitor lights up

Wink: Yes, PIP#2?

PIP#2: The boss of an electric company. A Chief Executive Officer. He or she is the big boss of the company, and wears a fancy suit to work, and tells all the workers what to do.

Audience laughter

Wink: You guessed it! Chief Executive Officer is what we were looking for. Sounds like you know a lot about that job. Perhaps you are headed toward that very career yourself, PIP#2. Pull that lever!

The lever is pulled. The audience yells, "No stinky diaper, no stinky diaper!"

Up come the pictures of Couple#3, Couple#3, Couple#1.

Wink: Oh, almost a clean sweep there, but you've earned a lot of points toward Couple#3.

Couple#3 clap and look at each other hopefully.

Wink: Now, this is the last question of this round before our bonus round. Listen carefully. This one is tricky.

Flashing lights, children, headache.

There is a pause.

Wink: Once again. Flashing lights, children, headache.

PIP#1 monitor lights up.

Wink: PIP#1, this may be your chance to get back in to the game. What occupation do you think these three items in the list indicate?

PIP#1: I'm not sure but, a school bus driver?

Wink: Yes indeed! A noble occupation indeed. Now pull that lever, and hopefully get back on the board.

The lever is pulled. Pictures of Couple #2, Couple #2, Couple #2

Audience cheers

Wink: Three in a row! Well, that mishap a few moments ago doesn't seem to have hurt you too badly – you've earned an amazing 1500 points toward Couple#2, plus, Johnny, tell PIP#1 what he has won.

Off-Camera Announcer: Well, PIP#1 you've won a lifetime supply of patience. You can draw on it when you need it, whether it be with your parents, teachers, siblings, whenever, and it will never run out. Congratulations!

Audience applause

Wink: Very nice indeed. We're at the end of Round Three – let's check the score board to see where everyone stands before we enter the all important bonus round.

Wink walks over to PIP#1 monitor

Wink: PIP#1, you have 1500 points toward Couple#2, and no points toward the other couples. That is looking like a match, but we all know everything can change in the bonus round.

Wink steps over to PIP#2 monitor

Wink: Will PIP#2 be matched with Couple#3? S/he has a hefty 2000 points toward them. The next round will tell.

Wink indicates PIP#3 monitor

Wink: PIP#3, let's see where you are on the scoreboard. Looks like the bulk of your points are toward Couple#2, putting you and PIP#1 tied for Couple#2's affections at this point. What an exciting game we have here!
We'll be back right after these messages to see who's going home with whom! Don't go away!

Audience applause

COMMERCIAL BREAK

Wink: Welcome back. We are about to pose our bonus question, for which all point values are doubled.

Close up of the three couples.

Wink: The parents are getting excited to know which bundle of joy they can be expecting soon.

Close up on the three PIP monitors

Wink: And the Persons in Progress are wondering which set of parents they'll be calling theirs in just a few moments. Remember, we're playing for keeps here, people!

Audience laughter

Drum Roll

Audience quiets

Wink: And now the bonus question. This will be the last and most important question of the day. The first PIP to light up and answer this question correctly gets the last pull of the lever, and the destiny of all our players will be determined. As the answer to this question will be subjective, we will turn to our judges to determine if your answer is worthy of a lever pull. Listen carefully please. Here is today's bonus question:

There is a chance that at least one of you may live this life as an individual with special needs. Would you embrace the situation, and why?

Pause

PIP#3 monitor lights up

Wink: PIP#3 was first to light up.

PIP#3: That's a tough question Wink, but I'm going to say yes, even though it would mean facing challenges that I can't now even imagine, I would embrace it. And I guess it wouldn't matter the nature or label of the specific challenge I would face, I would hope that it would open my eyes and the eyes of those around me to the need for compassion toward each other. I think that's about it...

Wink: Pip#3, you have spoken –

PIP#3: Oh, forgive me Wink, there's something else. Do we have time?

Wink: Please continue, by all means.

PIP#3: I think I would also appreciate my accomplishments all the more because of having to work so much harder to reach them.

Wink: Do you have anything else to add?

PIP#3: Well, just because my perspective on this world might be different from others', it doesn't mean my perspective would be wrong. Or bad. Or unfortunate. It would just be different. So, yes, Wink, I think I would embrace it. Thank you.

Pause

Audience is silent

Wink swallows hard

Wink: Well, suffice it to say that I don't need the nod from the judges to know that your very articulate and heartfelt answer has earned you the final pull of the day. Very well said, PIP#3. I'm sure you'll make any of the parents here today very proud. Now pull that lever! And remember, points are doubled! And don't pull up the stinky diaper!

PIP#3 pulls

Tense faces in the audience and on the panel of parents

Pictures of Couple#1, Couple#1, the audience gasps, and Couple#3

Disappointed sigh from the audience

Wink: Oh, so close to three in a row! But look at all the points you racked up on that pull. Let's take a look at the scoreboard and see how that double points pull altered the scores, and who is going home with whom at the end of today's show!

Close up on the scoreboard and the final scores.

Wink: And Ladies and Gentleman, the final scores are in, and here are today's matches!

Drum roll

Audience applause

Wink: It looks like PIP#1 is going home with Couple#2, with 1500 points toward them! PIP#2 has the most points, 2000 of them, toward Couple#3! And it looks like PIP#3, the big scorer in the bonus round, is destined to be with Couple #1!

Parents are ecstatic, and bounce up and down in their seats and embrace their spouses. The PIPs' monitors glow with bright colours. The audience hoots and cheers. The parents switch seats so that they are positioned in the chair behind their particular PIP, and they touch the monitor lovingly.

Wink: Ladies and Gentlemen, look at the happy faces of those expectant parents! As you can see, everyone's a winner here on First Comes Love. What a marvelous game here today! I just know that the matches we have made here today will result in a lot of happiness.

Goodnight everybody. Join us next time when three different Couples and three different Persons in Progress answer skill-testing questions and get in the family way! Thank you everyone! Goodnight! And remember, we're playing for keeps here, people!

Audience clapping and chanting:

> *First comes love!*
>
> *Then comes marriage!*
>
> *Then comes a bundle in a baby carriage!*

Audience applauds loudly as....

Credits roll

Mother's Day

Our Age of Innocence – A Screenplay

ACT ONE

FADE IN:

1. Interior. Overton living room – Evening

We PAN ACROSS *the room and settle on the sofa table, on which sits a nicely framed black-and-white photograph of* JENNIFER *holding a six-week-old baby* (NICHOLAS). *In the photo* JENNIFER *holds him up over her shoulder so that he faces the camera; a startled look on his face. Lots of dark, long hair standing on end, resembling a six-week-old Beethoven.* JENNIFER *is kissing his cheek. The* CREDITS ROLL *as we hear the sound of baby gurgling and baby talk...*

2. Exterior. Overton garden – Morning

We PAN ACROSS *the yard to the vegetable garden. Four-month-old baby* NICHOLAS *sits contentedly in a stroller beside the garden while* JENNIFER, *a thirty-something trim woman, pulls carrots from the soil and places them in a garden basket.*

JENNIFER

Oh yeah...a little steaming, a few turns in the food processor and...lunch.

3.   Interior. Overton kitchen – Evening

Four-month-old NICHOLAS *jumps happily in a jolly jumper hung in doorway between the kitchen and living room.* DAVID OVERTON, *a quiet, prematurely graying, sophisticated man in his late forties, sits at the kitchen table sipping a scotch.* JENNIFER *is busy making dinner. Broadway show tunes can be heard coming from the stereo in the living room.*

> DAVID (*watching* NICHOLAS *jump*
> *and kick*)
> Go, Nic, go!(To JENNIFER) Y' know, he kind of reminds me of Pinocchio, trying to dance, become a real boy.

> JENNIFER (*laughing*)
> Yeah, remember when we first put him in there – he hated it.

> JENNIFER *is now taking the roast out of the roasting pan. She opens the drawer and gets the tin foil out; rips off a sheet.* BABY NICHOLAS *screams at the top of his lungs.* DAVID *and* JENNIFER *stare at each other in amazement. They rush to* BABY NICHOLAS *to see why he has screamed. The sound of screaming underscores the transition into the next scene.*

4.   Interior. Martha Irving's kitchen – Morning

Baby NICHOLAS *on his back on a baby quilt on the floor in the middle of the kitchen, happily swatting at toys hanging from a baby gym.* JENNIFER *and* MARTHA, *an attractive artistic woman in her early thirties, sit at a large oak country table.* MARTHA *pours tea.*

> MARTHA
> So, what's it like?

> JENNIFER
> You know, all-consuming.

MARTHA

He's so gorgeous. Can I hold him?

JENNIFER

Go for it.

MARTHA *goes over to* NICHOLAS *and gently picks him up.* NICHOLAS *screams and stiffens.* MARTHA *struggles to hold him and tries speaking soothingly to him. He continues to scream.* MARTHA *hands him over to* JENNIFER. NICHOLAS *remains upset but less so. As* JENNIFER *tries to comfort him...*

JENNIFER

He's a bit shy I guess. He doesn't like to be held by anyone but me. And not always by me. (*Trying to laugh it off.*) Don't take it personally – he's tired.

JENNIFER *hands* NICHOLAS *a plastic baby book of black and white shapes and faces. He immediately quiets. He sits propped up on her lap.*

MARTHA

I never noticed the dimple in his chin before. I guess that's where God touched him and marked him as a special boy.

JENNIFER *looks down at* NICHOLAS *with pride. Special indeed.* MARTHA *tries to make him smile with baby talk.*

5. Interior. Barber shop – Day

A nineteen-fifties style barber shop, complete with leather barber chairs and barber pole. DAVID *sits in a barber chair with four-month-old* NICHOLAS *held in his lap. They both wear smocks.* JENNIFER *stands beside them with a video camera. A small woman in her mid-forties* (NANCY) *stands behind the chair, removing her comb and scissors from her smock.*

NANCY

I don't know. I gotta tell ya I'm a little nervous. I've never cut a four-month-old's hair before.

JENNIFER

Well it's cute and all, but he's been having a lot of bad hair days lately, if you know what I mean. They told me at the hospital that he would lose it all soon after he was born, but I've been checking his crib, and not one hair has fallen out! (*She laughs.*)

DAVID

Yeah, I guess it's time.

> JENNIFER *holds up the video camera. The rest of the scene is realistic video coverage, from* JENNIFER'S *point of view.* NANCY *gently pulls up a piece of hair on top of* NICHOLAS' *head and cuts it with her scissors. She hands it to* DAVID *who places it in a small plastic bag. As* NANCY *pulls up the next bit of hair, we see the reflected image of* JENNIFER *holding the video camera in the mirror...*

JENNIFER

Smile, my big boy! Who's my big boy getting his first haircut?

6.   Interior. Doctor's office – Day

> DR. CARLOS, *a friendly efficient woman in her late forties, writes notes while* JENNIFER *dresses* NICHOLAS, *now six months old.*

DR. CARLOS

He's in the ninetieth and eightieth percentiles for height and weight. You said he sleeps and eats well. Is he happy?

JENNIFER

Seems to be. He's very easy, not demanding.

DR. CARLOS

Oh, just wait until he starts moving around. Now, I know the pregnancy was difficult. How are you doing now?

JENNIFER

Pretty good I guess. I've just agreed to teach a half course at the university. Works out perfectly with Nicholas' schedule. I'll breastfeed him, drive him to my friend's house, he'll nap while I teach, I pick him up, we're home. Only two mornings a week.

CUT TO:

7. Interior. Overton living room - Day

Eleven-month old NICHOLAS *cruises (walking) around the coffee table, then plops down and turns toy cars over and spins the wheels. A sea of toys. He only has eyes for his car. Raffi music on the stereo.* JENNIFER *is watering plants. She sings along with the music.* NICHOLAS *is oblivious to her, absorbed in his toy car.*

JENNIFER

Hey you almost walker, you, how about learning to crawl, hmm? Like your friend Melissa.

She takes away his car. He starts to scream and cry, trying to get it back. Like his heart had just been ripped out. JENNIFER *takes the car and puts it on the other side of the room. Puts* NICHOLAS *on his knees, and encourages him to get the car. He just screams and sits. She puts him on his knees again. Again he sits, and continues to scream.*

JENNIFER

Do you want the car? C'mon, Nic. Go and get it!

She models for him, crawling across the room. Still nothing. She puts him on his hands and knees, and places her hands physically on his hand and moves it forward, then a knee, then the other hand, other knee, etc. He screams bloody murder. She is clearly frazzled. He sits on the floor. She sits beside him, looking at him with concern.

8.   Interior. Overton dining room - Night

Dinner dishes being cleared from the table by DAVID. NICHOLAS *in pajamas lying on the floor, twirling a leaf he found earlier in the day and has held ever since. Beside him is his tape recorder. He lies quietly listening to the music, not interested in anything else.* JENNIFER *writes in his baby book.* CLOSE UP *on baby book as she writes…*

Saying words at 10 months: Hi; bye; tickle-tickle; doggie; night-night; dada; mama; baby. We might hear them only once. But little interest in getting anywhere. We've learned not to spend a lot of money on toys for you as your favourite toys are inevitably things like the lid from the yogurt container, a piece of yellow wool, a leaf, a twig, a handkerchief which you drape over your head, a blade of grass, and of course, your beloved blankie. Oh, and yes, I must have been mistaken, but the other day I swear I heard you recite the days of the week! You're not even one yet!

PAN OVER *to* NICHOLAS *listening to music, contentedly twirling his leaf.*

9.   Interior. Overton living room - Night

TRACK SHOT *through the kitchen and dining room to the living room. There we find* NICHOLAS *in his highchair, balloons everywhere, a paper party hat askew on his one-year-old head. He is screaming and crying.* JENNIFER *and* DAVID, *also wearing party hats, are holding a birthday cake with one big candle in the center. They are singing Happy Birthday over* NICHOLAS' *screams. When they stop singing,* NICHOLAS *stops screaming. They blow out the candle for him and cut the cake. Carrot cake with cream cheese icing. He loves it. Gifts are piled on the table.* JENNIFER *starts to unwrap them.* NICHOLAS *screams at the sound of the gift paper ripping.* CUT TO:

10. Interior. Doctors office

DR. CARLOS *is loading a syringe with vaccination. During the conversation, she injects it into* NICHOLAS' *thigh.*

> DR. CARLOS
>
> Well, you are a big strapping boy! OK, Nicholas, this is going to sting a little bit...give him some Tylenol if he gets warm. (*TO* NICHOLAS) No, I know, you're not going to want to come see Dr. Ann if that's what she's going to do to you, are you?

> JENNIFER
>
> What does MMR stand for?

> DR. CARLOS
>
> Measles, mumps, rubella.

> FADE OUT *on* NICHOLAS *crying and* JENNIFER *trying to soothe him.*

11. Interior. Shopping mall

A frazzled young woman dressed as Santa's helper setting up a camera in 'Santa's Village' in the mall. A lineup of noisy youngsters with parents. Cheesy Christmas music playing.

CUT TO:

12. Photograph

A Christmas photo of NICHOLAS *on Santa's knee.* NICHOLAS *is very cute, dressed in jeans and suspenders and bow tie; thick mop of hair makes him resemble one of the Beatles; he holds his blankie. His face and body language reveal a toddler in serious distress: his face shows fear and anxiety; he is in the process of wriggling out of Santa's arms when the picture was snapped. Santa, however, exemplifies an aura of "I've seen it all" boredom. This is not a typical happy Christmas memory photo.* CUT TO:

13. Interior. Overton bedroom - Morning

A gorgeous eighteen-month-old NICHOLAS *in pajamas and* DAVID *in sweatshirt and trackpants lie on* JENNIFER *and* DAVID'S *bed with a stack of books beside them. Weekend morning. Lazy. Early spring.* DAVID *and* NICHOLAS *are looking at a book of farm animals.* NICHOLAS *is making the sounds of the animals. They read a book about body parts, and* DAVID *asks him where his various body parts are, and he points to them.* TRACK SHOT *through the house following* NICHOLAS *as he toddles out of the bedroom and into the living room, to a clock which is just winding down. He points to it and grunts.* DAVID *comes out of the bedroom:*

> DAVID

Clock Police. Yes, I'll wind it.

> TRACK SHOT *of* NICHOLAS *running through house, turning on all the lights, counting them as he does it.*

> NICHOLAS

One, two, three, four, five, six, seven, eight, nine, ten.

> *He runs through the house, opening all the doors.* CUT TO: JENNIFER *in the kitchen, closing the back door as she has just come in from emptying the trash.* NICHOLAS *immediately comes running in to the kitchen, crying, and runs to the back door and opens it.*

> JENNIFER

Oh, right. They all have to be open, or all closed – I forgot.

> TRACK SHOT *of* NICHOLAS *running in to his room and plopping into his beanbag chair with his book of numbers.* FADE OUT.

14. Interior. Car - Day

JENNIFER *driving,* NICHOLAS *in car seat in back seat.*

                              JENNIFER
Yes, you're going to get a big boy haircut! Linda's going to do
it for you this time, not me, and she's doing it at her house.
You're going to look so handsome at your birthday party! Yes!

> CLOSE UP *on* NICHOLAS *in back seat, pointing out the*
> *window to traffic signs and signals, and saying "stop sign," "red*
> *light" etc.* CUT TO:

15. Interior. Home basement salon – Day

> *A makeshift hair salon in the basement of* LINDA, *a crisp, entrepreneurial*
> *type with last decade's hair style.* JENNIFER *plops* NICHOLAS *onto the*
> *board across the chair.* LINDA *places a smock around his neck.*

                              LINDA
So, what are we doing today?

                              JENNIFER
I was thinking, can you do one of those cute mushroom cuts?

                              LINDA
Sure thing.

                              JENNIFER
Do you do that with scissors, or clippers?

                              LINDA
I start with clippers around the bottom, then scissors for the
top.

                              JENNIFER
Oh, Nic, clippers! That's a first for you – you're gonna look
just like a big boy!

> *She starts the clippers.* NICHOLAS *freaks out: screaming,*
> *crying, flailing arms and legs, covering his ears.* JENNIFER *is*
> *clearly surprised and concerned. This is beyond typical tears or*

being scared. LINDA *looks to* JENNIFER *in a "well, what do you want me to do?" look.*

JENNIFER
Well you've started. Let's finish it.

JENNIFER *holds* NICHOLAS *down as* LINDA, *clearly uncomfortable, goes about the business of cutting his hair as quickly as she can.* NICHOLAS *screams and fights throughout.* CUT TO:

16. Interior. Car – Moments later

NICHOLAS *in his car seat, still sobbing, with a mushroom cut. He's mad.* JENNIFER *sits in the driver's seat, confused, apologetic tears welling up in her eyes. She looks in the rearview mirror to* NICHOLAS.

JENNIFER (whispering)
I just wanted you to look nice for your party...

17. Exterior. Overton house – Day

Guests arriving for NICHOLAS' *second birthday party. Toddlers and parents arrive with gifts. The yard is decorated with balloons and streamers. Toddlers run for the slide and swings, giggling and chatting. Newspaper and pumpkins litter the patio table – jack-o-lanterns will be made.* NICHOLAS *is nowhere to be seen. Storm clouds are gathering in the autumn sky.*

18. Interior. Overton house – Day

TRACKING SHOT *through the house. Kids laughing, playing, parents chatting in each of the rooms of the bungalow. A* PARENT *is heard to say, "Where's the birthday boy?" and "Where's Nicholas?" as the camera tracks through the guests. To* NICHOLAS' BEDROOM, *where the door is shut, and when opened,* NICHOLAS *is discovered under the covers of his bed, playing with his alphabet blocks.*

19. Interior. Living room - Day

All the party guests gathered around, eating cake and ice cream. The room decorated in a train theme. Kids wanting NICHOLAS *to open the presents they brought.* NICHOLAS *is in a corner, twirling a piece of ribbon in his hands.*

> JENNIFER

C'mon, Nic, let's open presents.

No response from NICHOLAS.

> JENNIFER

C'mon, I'll help you...

> JENNIFER *goes to him and tries to pick him up. He screams and wriggles free. She takes him by the hand. He flops to the floor and starts banging his head on the carpet.* JENNIFER *looks sheepishly to the wide-eyed guests.* HOLD ON JENNIFER.

> JENNIFER

He must be tired...

20. Interior. Doctor's waiting room - Day

The door opens as JENNIFER *and a reluctant* NICHOLAS *enter. He screams and runs out.* JENNIFER *retrieves him several times.* NICHOLAS *does not want to go in there. The* NURSE *calls his name to accompany her to the doctor's office.* JENNIFER *tries to coax him to come, but he refuses. Finally* JENNIFER *decides to go back herself, hoping he will follow her.*

21. Interior. Doctor's office

JENNIFER *sits uncomfortably in a chair, holding a box of raisins.* NICHOLAS *can still be heard screaming in the waiting room.*

JENNIFER

(*TO* DR. CARLOS) He seems so...sensitive. And ever since I took him to get his hair cut, he refuses to enter anyone's home or office. Was it that traumatic for him? It was just a haircut – kids have them all the time!

DR. CARLOS

That kind of sensitivity probably means that he's smart. How is his talking coming along?

JENNIFER

Well, he's talking. It's unique, not like his little friends. He kind of echoes what I say. Like he'll come into the kitchen and say, "Do you want some juice?" And that means he wants juice.

> NICHOLAS *toddles into* DR. CARLOS *office, tantrum almost over, and walks toward the blood pressure machine and touches it.*

NICHOLAS

That's not to touch. That's precious and delicate.

DR. CARLOS

Yes, it is, Nicholas. What's your name?

NICHOLAS

N-I-C-H-O-L-A-S O-V-E-R-T-O-N, 283 Brookside Road. B3T 1T2. 852-2993

JENNIFER

He always spells out his name when asked.

> NICHOLAS *sees a book of shapes. He opens it. Gets excited and flaps his hands.*

NICHOLAS

Octagon! Triangle! Circle!

DR. CARLOS

See? He's smart.

22. Interior. Overton home - Evening

Sound of Wheel of Fortune theme coming from the living room TV as JENNIFER *enters the kitchen door, carrying groceries.* CAMERA PANS DOWN *to what she sees on the floor: a line of plates extending from the kitchen into the dining room. She places the groceries on the counter and makes her way toward the living room, stepping around the plates in the dining room. There she sees* DAVID *reading and* NICHOLAS *watching* Wheel of Fortune. *He is absorbed and excited, calling out the letters as they are turned. He is oblivious to his mother's arrival. On the bay window sill is a line of cups, arranged according to size. On the floor are lined up cans from the pantry. She checks the cans, and sure enough, they are lined up alphabetically.*

JENNIFER (to herself as she reads the can labels)

Applesauce, beans, corn...

A disturbed smile crosses her face, as she tries to get NICHOLAS' *attention to greet him.* JENNIFER *and* DAVID *share a look.*

23. Interior. Overton kitchen - Day

JENNIFER *is talking on the phone, while* NICHOLAS *plays with his alphabet blocks, reciting the letters.*

JENNIFER

I know it's the terrible twos, Mom, but did any of us bang our heads when we were mad? I mean, he never actually hurts himself, he does it on the carpet, but it's getting really frequent. (*Pause*) Yeah, I've got us registered to start Moms and Tots. (*Pause*) Yeah, maybe the social thing will help. But hey, you know what he did yesterday? He brought a twig into the house and gave it to me and said "Kind of like an R" and you know what, when I turned it around, it did look like a small R. Isn't that something? Oh, gotta go, my bread is done. (*Pause*) Soon. Love you too. Bye.

She hangs up the phone and talks to NICHOLAS.
Oma sends you her biggest Oma hug. Nicholas. Nicholas!

No response from NICHOLAS, *who is totally absorbed in his blocks.*

24. Interior. Community center - Day

A gym with different activity centers. Mats with toys, a trampoline, a craft area with paper and crayons. Moms and Tots morning program. Noisy, bustling. JENNIFER *and* NICHOLAS *enter and begin to remove jackets. A* TODDLER *runs over to say hi,* NICHOLAS *strikes out at him.* JENNIFER *apologizes to the boy, begins a tour of the facility with* NICHOLAS. *Kids running all around.* NICHOLAS *appears frightened. Not talking. A* MOM *brings her daughter over to introduce themselves,* NICHOLAS *takes off and begins to run around the outside wall of the gymnasium. Lap after lap, with no response when* JENNIFER *calls to him. He stops only when all the others have retreated to the craft area.*

JENNIFER
Nicholas, it's craft time. Come and colour on the paper.

NICHOLAS
No!

Dragging NICHOLAS *to the craft table, determined to have him fit in with the other kids.*

JENNIFER
C'mon, sit here and I'll get paper and crayons.

NICHOLAS *throws the paper and all the crayons he can get his hands on. Glances between parents.* NICHOLAS *turns to the child next to him, hits her.*

NICHOLAS

Now cry!

Appalled, JENNIFER *takes him away from the table.*

JENNIFER

Nicholas! That is not nice! Now let's go colour — and you be nice to the other kids!

NICHOLAS *runs to the mats and repeatedly bangs his head on the mat. All the parents and tots are watching.* JENNIFER *is burning with confusion and humiliation. Apparently socializing him was not going to be as easy or make him like other kids as much as she had hoped. Deep concern in her eyes. An attempt at a wavering smile.*

JENNIFER

I guess he's a watcher, not a doer. He has his own way of playing with toys.

25. Interior. Car. Community Center Parking Lot

A crying JENNIFER *sits slumped over the steering wheel.* NICHOLAS *in his car seat in the back seat, indifferent to her emotional state, looking at the traffic signals at a nearby intersection.*

NICHOLAS

Red light. Green light. Red light. Yellow light.

26. Interior. Overton kitchen — Day

JENNIFER *has the phone book open in front of her and the Nova Scotia Speech and Language Clinic is underlined. She talks on the phone.*

JENNIFER

Well, for instance, he doesn't say "I". He refers to himself as "Nicholas". (*Pause*) Yes, he's two and a half. (*Pause*) It's common is it? Another thing. I wonder if he might have a hearing problem. Sometimes I have a lot of trouble getting his attention. (*Pause*) Uh huh. So I shouldn't worry. OK. Thank you.

> *She hangs up the phone and looks at* NICHOLAS, *who is jumping up and down on the bathroom scale he has brought into the kitchen, watching the numbered dial rotate as he jumps on it, shouting with glee:*

NICHOLAS

Wheel of Fortune!

> CLOSE UP *on* JENNIFER'S *face, filled with wanting to believe nothing is wrong with her beautiful son, but the nagging concerns lingering, even after her conversation with the Speech and Language Clinic.* HOLD ON HER EYES AS SHE WATCHES HER SON.

27. Interior. Doctor's office – Day

A middle-aged, brisk female doctor (DR. REBUS) *sits at her desk, looking over* NICHOLAS' *file.*

DR. REBUS

Dr. Carlos left excellent notes. He certainly looks healthy.

She examines his eyes and nose and ears.

JENNIFER

I'm, well, I'm a little concerned. He's my only, so I don't have a point of comparison, but he seems to be different from his peers...

DR. REBUS (*briskly*)

How so?

JENNIFER

Well, he doesn't seem interested in making friends.

DR. REBUS
Remember, he's a boy...

JENNIFER
His talking is...well, different from other kids. I don't know.
He gets easily upset. He likes things a certain way.

DR. REBUS
Is his language increasing?

JENNIFER
Yes, but he doesn't seem interested in learning about things
other than numbers and letters, like toilet training for
instance. And yet, I walked into his room the other day, and
there was the word "chicken" spelled out with his alphabet
blocks. But when I ask him to get dressed, or pick up his toys,
he either doesn't look up, or if he does, he looks at me like he
doesn't know what I'm talking about.

DR. REBUS
He's smart — he's probably trying to push your buttons.

She looks at NICHOLAS *playing in the corner of her office.*
Three seconds later:
He's fine. You're worrying too much. Go home and enjoy
him.

SNAP TO BLACK. SNAP UP:

28. Interior. Doctor's office – Day

Four months later. Still DR. CARLOS *is on leave.* DR. REBUS, *wearing*
different clothes and hair style, bustles through the door with NICHOLAS'
file in her hands. NICHOLAS *and* JENNIFER *have been waiting there for*
some time. NICHOLAS *will not be held any longer.*

DR. REBUS
And how is Nicholas today? Cold? Flu?

JENNIFER

No, he's fine. Physically. Listen, I may be a worrier, but I'm really concerned about him. About the things we talked about last time. Last week he poked me in the eye, and laughed as I cried in pain. He didn't even care that I was hurt.

DR.REBUS (trying to hide her impatience)

He's testing your limits. Be firm with him. He's a big beautiful healthy child. Boys take their own time with things. Try not to worry so much.

> HOLD ON NICHOLAS *in the corner of the office making letters with Q tips: V, W. In his own world.* SNAP TO:

29. Interior. Doctor's office – Day

Five months later. NICHOLAS *is almost three and a half years old. Clearly worried and uncomfortable,* JENNIFER, *hair longer and face drawn, sits in* DR. REBUS' *office yet again to discuss* NICHOLAS' *development.* NICHOLAS, *bigger, sits on* JENNIFER's *lap, playing with her calculator, absorbed in watching the numbers come up on the calculator's screen.* JENNIFER *is near tears.*

JENNIFER

...I just don't know what to do or who to talk to...

DR. REBUS (losing patience)

Look. His file indicates that this is the third time you've come with concerns. If you are still so worried, I'll make an appointment for Nicholas at the Developmental Clinic at the hospital. If only to put your mind at ease.

> *She grabs a form from her desk drawer and begins to fill it out.*

I should warn you though, they have a long waiting list. It may be a while before you get seen.

> HOLD ON NICHOLAS *in* JENNIFER'S *lap, playing with the calculator, oblivious to the events surrounding him.* JENNIFER

looks at him with love and worry. Why couldn't she just believe
DR. REBUS? *Why does she worry so much? Does she really*
want to go there — the Developmental Clinic — what if they find
something seriously wrong with him? She knows she has to go
there.

30. Interior. Overton living room - Night

DAVID *and* JENNIFER *sitting on the couch. The TV is on but muted.*

> DAVID

So, I guess a private psychologist could look at him sooner
than the hospital?

> JENNIFER

Yeah. But I wouldn't know where to begin to look for one.
And does our insurance cover that?

> DAVID

I'll check tomorrow.

> *He grabs the remote from the table.*

Is this it?

> JENNIFER

Yeah. I saw an ad that this was on tonight. I... I don't know. I
just want to see it.

> *The TV gets unmuted. On the television we see the show's title:*
> *The Nature of Things with* DAVID SUZUKI. *The host,* DAVID
> SUZUKI, *appears on the screen to introduce the program.*

> DAVID SUZUKI (*on TV*)

A child who doesn't know how to play. May not have many
communication skills. Lacks eye contact with others. Autism.
This baffling disorder...

> *As* DAVID SUZUKI *continues to narrate, video footage of two*
> *autistic four-year-old twin boys appears on the screen. They do*

not relate to one another. They are surrounded by toys, but don't play with them, preferring to walk around in ritualistic patterns, flapping their hands and emitting high-pitched screeches, and mumbling.

CLOSE UP on JENNIFER *as the recognition happens. The sound on the TV blurs as we see* JENNIFER'S *face dissolve into the realization of what is wrong with her son. All the months and years of concern collide in her, as she sees* NICHOLAS *in these twin boys. Tears roll down her otherwise immobile face.*

JENNIFER (barely audible)
That's him. That's our son.

Tears stream down her face. This is a flood that will continue for many days to come. HOLD ON JENNIFER. SLOW FADE TO BLACK.

END OF ACT ONE.

Moving Day

Great Expectations

Before Nicholas was born, I went to an exclusive baby store and bought a fancy, expensive, leather-bound baby book. The cover was embossed with gold calligraphy, and the pages were adorned with drawings of antique teddy bears and dolls. It was adorable.

It was going to be the repository for recording all the perfect milestones and perfect memories and perfect photos of Nicholas' perfect babyhood. It included pages for filling in his family tree, his height, his weight, his vaccinations, his christening, his first sit up, his first independent step, his first words, his playmates, his birthday party guests, his early school years. One of the pages even housed a silk pocket in which to store a precious lock of hair from his first haircut. One of the things I liked most about the book was that it contained plenty of space for both formal photographs and candid snapshots.

I was determined that it would be a carefully attended-to chronicle of, and tribute to, his childhood. A summary glimpse of his early life. His formative years.

I suppose I took such care because the only record of my early years was an entry in the family Bible announcing my birth. I wanted more for my child.

In addition to all the statistics I would enter, I looked forward to composing and writing comments about his childhood that would capture his imagination when he was older, and provide fodder for embarrassing moments in front of teenage girlfriends: bare-bum pictures, funny stories, witty remarks, and observations about his developing personality.

It was my plan that this special book would be looked at and cherished by him, be enjoyed by his children, and get passed down from generation to generation. A keepsake.

It was eight years ago that I purchased that baby book, that I invested in that dream.

I came across it recently while unpacking the last of our boxes from our move to our current home. My heart skipped a beat when I saw it.

I paused before carefully lifting it from the box. I wiped off the cover with my sleeve. I paused again before tentatively opening it to the first page. There it was: the photo of our smiling, exhausted faces as we held him, our son, a newborn in my arms.

On the following page was an inventory of his birth statistics, including the name of the doctor who helped deliver him, and a copy of his birth certificate.

I skipped through the pages of carefully catalogued first-year milestones and anecdotes to the page that held his first birthday photo: a beautiful boy sitting in his highchair, party hat askew on his head, carrot cake and cream cheese icing all over his face. David and I are posed behind him, smiling. The perfect middle-class couple with their perfect only son.

I flipped through more memory-filled pages and photographs that revealed our joy, our celebrations, our hopes, our dreams.

Oh yes – and our innocence.

Looking at them now, in retrospect, some of the photos seem strained, too perfect. Looking at them now, I appear to be smiling too hard in those pictures, almost as if I'm trying to dismiss my growing concern about my beautiful son. Cover it up. Smile it away. Looking at them now, those written entries reveal, between the lines, an attempt to convince myself that his unusual behaviour was merely eccentricity or laziness.

I turned to his second birthday photo. An even more beautiful boy, sitting in an antique child's rocker, wearing a homemade cardigan with teddy bear buttons, bow tie at his throat, holding tight to Barney in one arm and his blankie in the other. Smiling shyly. Looking right at the camera. Perfect. Handsome. Healthy.

And then nothing. No more photos. No more writing. No more entries of any kind. Nothing but blank page after blank page. Abrupt. Empty. Vacant.

What had started out as a cherished archive of babyhood mementos: the date of each new tooth, each new sound, each reach and wiggle on the road of his childhood; the childhood we thought he was having, the childhood we had hoped for and held dear; came to a sudden halt. Just stopped. And then nothing.

Overnight, our ordered world turned to chaos. We had slipped, unnoticed, down the rabbit hole. Into the land of autism.

My puddling tears are the only marks on those otherwise untouched pages.

I placed the book gently back in the box.

Father's Day

Heirloom

When I was seventeen or eighteen, I remember spotting what looked like a gold ring buried in my father's cufflink box. I asked him about it, and he said, "Oh, yes. That's the family ring. It belonged to your grandfather, and when he died, I got it."

I looked at it closely and asked him what he knew about the image on its face: a bird sitting on what looked like a crown. "Oh," he said, "it's all heraldry. It's symbolic. It means Lord Overton went out and had a lark with the Queen."

He then went on with a story about how the ring had been passed down from father to first son for generations, a story with numerous embellishments and flourishes. I knew how my father liked to add some colour to the truth of his stories, so I listened with a large grain of salt. A year or so later, when it was obvious to me that he would never wear the ring, I asked if he'd mind if I wore it. I've worn it ever since.

In the late sixties, during one of those genealogy crazes that comes along every so often, when people were having their family crests researched and painted, my parents discovered that the image on the ring really was the crest of a particular branch of the family. Not a lark on a crown at all, of course, but a martlet on a chapeau. So much for Lord Overton and his royal escapades. It also turned out that the bird and chapeau were backwards on the ring. Of course, I realized – it's a seal ring. But I still believed my grandfather had had the ring made, probably during some earlier genealogy craze of the twenties or thirties.

Later I met an antique jewelry specialist who looked at the marks inside the ring and assured me that it was much older than I believed, dating from the middle of the eighteenth century. Well, I thought, maybe there's something to the old man's story after all. If you didn't pay too much attention to the merry adventures of the mythical Lord Overton.

And there was something rather appealing and reassuring in the image: an unbroken line of heredity stretching back to before the days of the American and French revolutions. Patriarchal, to be sure, with its adherence to male primogeniture, but there was no particularly compelling reason why that part of the tradition had to continue. When we learned Jennifer was pregnant, we were both convinced that it was a daughter we would be having, to the extent that when Nicholas was born, we had only picked out girls' names. When Nic surprisingly emerged into our lives that October night, it created a highly compelling reason for the continuance of the male birthright: the only child in the line of inheritance was a son.

And here's the twist: he's a son who's highly unlikely to have any interest in the rituals of courtship and reproduction that would lead to passing on this heirloom. Socially awkward and unconcerned with the niceties of interpersonal conventions, we realize that Nic is unlikely to marry or even have a serious relationship. He's the last of the Mohicans, this one. "Just nature taking care of itself," Jennifer will say as she watches the rain fall on her garden. Perhaps. Perhaps Nic's lack of sociability is the same.

And yet, there remains this ring. This ring with its mythical and real history, intertwined and perhaps inseparable now. It represents what's passed on from one generation to the next: an emblem of heredity, its markings as enigmantic and mysterious as those grey and black lines on a DNA chart. What is it we inherit, after all? Dominant and recessive traits. A tendency to fat or thin. Blue eyes or brown. Does your tongue curl? Those peculiar markers that stamp our individuality, set us off from the rest of humanity. Aunt Gladys' nose. Grandmother Hilda's bald spot. Your father's moustache.

What we inherit is a set of genes and a mythology. We search our family past for any signs that someone else might have shown signs of Nic's condition. How did they cope with it? Did they survive? Thrive? Genetic predisposition isn't that simple, after all. Nic and I share many traits, traits I shared with my forebears. Some difficulty with eye contact. A fascination with word and language games. A tendency to talk to imaginary companions. A desire to watch the world rather than participate. The question is not where they come from, but how he will be able to deal with them. How well will he cope with a world that may not entirely welcome his idiosyncrasies?

Nic wanders into my study. "Dad," he says, "I've got something to show you in the family room."

He takes my hand and leads me downstairs. His *Birds of North America* book is out and beside it he's drawn a picture. It's labeled "Great Blue Heron."

"Terrific picture," I say. "I really like the wings. Now, why do you suppose it's called a great blue heron?"

"Because it's blue and it's a heron. And it's great."

No arguing with that logic. I try to move the conversation away from his obsessive preoccupations, thinking about what I've just been writing.

"It looks a bit like this bird," I say, showing him the stylized image on the ring.

"Is that a heron?" he asks.

"No," I explain. "It's a different kind of bird. It's called a martlet. It's…"

"No, no!" he cries. "I don't want it to be a marklep. I want it to be a heron."

"Well," I say, "you know there are other kinds of birds. A martlet is…"

His hands begin to flap. "No," he cries. "It looks like a heron. I want it to be a heron."

Best to avoid escalation at this point. There'll be time for family history later. "OK," I say. "It does look a bit like a heron."

"I'm going to draw a picture of that heron," he says, pointing to the ring. "You can go back to work."

I return to my desk. For some reason, the Greek word "entelechy" pops into my head. "Entelechy" means something like the tendency of an organism to seek the complete and perfect expression of its own inherent nature. The acorn contains the will and the desire to become a particular oak tree, and, unless the lightning bolt or the woodcutter's axe intervenes, it will do so. And no matter how much we may try to change patterns of growth through the manipulation of limbs and branches, the tendency to return to the original pattern will always be there. It's what the tree inherited, along with the combination of markers that makes it unique.

Each morning, as I've grown older, I've looked in the mirror and wondered how my father got in there. I've inherited much about his face, his body, his stance, his manner of speech. But I'm not my father. Whatever I may have inherited, it's my own entelechy I'm seeking.

Nic brings me in his drawing of the "heron" on the ring. It's not a bad likeness – his eye is quick at taking in details and his retention of them is remarkable.

"Very nice," I remark. "What's that he's standing on?" I glance at the "chapeau" on the ring.

"It's some long grass," replies Nic. "Herons stand on long grass."

"I see. Excellent."

"It's for you," he says, ripping off a piece of tape and sticking the drawing on the wall. "For Father's Day." And then he's heading off down the stairs, calling back, "See ya."

Father's Day. Fathers and children. An unbroken line of inheritance, stretching back beyond the French and American revolutions into the dark mysteries of the past. And all of it culminating in this strange child, working so hard, despite the constant interference of his parents and the team of experts on his case, to find the perfection of his own unique nature, his own entelechy. What is he, I wonder? A lark on a crown? A martlet on a chapeau? A great blue heron on a patch of long grass? Well, what does it matter, after all? He is what he is, and I wouldn't have him any other way. Like all the rest of us caught in the web of genetics and mythologies, Nic will put his own unique spin on the family history.

After all – he's my boy.

June 21st: The End of the School Year

O Canada! We Stand on Guard for Thee

Nicholas simply will not wear shorts before June 21st, the official first day of summer.

No matter how hot and sticky the weather gets before June 21st, he refuses.

Conversely, no matter how cool and rainy June 21st is – not uncommon in Nova Scotia – he insists on wearing shorts, a tee shirt, sandals, and his ball cap. He has very rigid rules where seasonal dress is concerned.

Every year I pray that it doesn't snow before December 21st, the first official day of winter.

But here we are, June 21st, Nicholas in his shorts and sandals, me in my raincoat-covered housecoat, standing at the end of the driveway in the cool rain, waiting for the school bus.

He announces its arrival long before I can hear it, even before the dog can hear it, and we wait the thirty seconds or so until it comes into view.

And sure enough, he is the only child on the bus wearing summer clothing.

"Today is the first day of summer," he proudly announces, totally disregarding the bus driver's greeting. I remind him to say good morning to Brian and the kids on the bus.

"Good morning Brian, Carla, etcetera," he says, quickly scanning the faces on the bus.

He takes his seat beside one of the many boys wearing long pants and a jacket. Nic is oblivious to the fact that he is dressed differently from the others.

"Love you," I blow him a kiss. "Have a great day!" I wave as the bus pulls down the street.

I return inside to my now cold cup of tea, and begin preparations for David's and my morning exercise walk with the dog.

Dressed, I pull on my sneakers and windbreaker. I remember how Nicholas is dressed. I hope the sun comes out today. They must think I'm the worst mother on the planet, sending him to school dressed inappropriately like that. I'm sure the other kids go home and tell their parents about how poor Nicholas was shivering all day because his mother made him wear shorts to school on a cold wet day. I'm reassured by the fact that Nicholas doesn't seem to register heat or cold – it's as if his internal thermostat is different from ours. I've never heard him complain about being hot or cold, no matter what the weather, or what he is wearing.

Still, maybe I should take out an ad in the local newspaper or something explaining all of this. And run it four times a year when the seasons change.

After 'walkies' with David and Vanna the dog, I shower and ready myself for an audition I have that morning. David is going to be at the university in meetings all day.

I dress carefully, wanting to give the right impression. I look at the scene that was faxed to me yesterday, put a copy of my headshot and résumé into my bag, turn on the cell phone, kiss my husband goodbye, and get into the car.

As I drive into town, I go over and over my lines. I check my lipstick in the rearview mirror. I do a vocal warmup. Even though the car windows are rolled up, I get sometimes amused, sometimes horrified looks from the cars next to me at the traffic light.

I arrive at the audition and take a seat in the waiting area along with all the other middle-aged women, all of us hoping to get this job. I think to myself, I'm getting too old for this. To have to always audition again and again every time a job comes up – it's getting tiresome. And talent has so little to do with it. I may not get the job because my eyes are blue instead of brown, and this role requires someone with brown eyes. So many variables that are out of my control. I am definitely getting too old for this...

The woman ahead of me goes in. I'm up next. I reach into my bag and get my headshot and résumé so I won't be scrambling for it when my name is called. I turn off my cell phone. I smooth back my graying hair, going over in my mind what I will say when asked to tell them a little bit about myself.

The woman ahead of me comes out smiling weakly and trembling. Not a good sign.

My name is called. As I stand up, I check in with all the places in my body that are holding tension, and send them a command to relax. A deep breath. A smile. I walk confidently in.

The next few minutes are a blur of introductions, acting the scene in front of the camera (the person reading the other part apparently just having learned to read), the director directing me to do it a completely different way, and thank-yous.

I leave the room smiling weakly and trembling. Oh well, there's always the next part...

Since Nicholas is at school and David at meetings, I have no reason to hurry home. And there is a new store that has opened up downtown, and I figure I'll treat myself to a bit of lunch and a luxurious window shop.

I walk leisurely down Spring Garden Road, popping into bookstores and boutiques. I stop for lunch at a deli and indulge in a huge sandwich bursting with every sandwich ingredient imaginable.

Walking back up Spring Garden toward the car, I bump into a friend I haven't seen in months. I check the clock over the library door. I have plenty of time to get back to the house to meet Nicholas' bus, so we slide into a coffee shop and have a great chat.

I return to the car and drive the twenty minutes to our home outside of town.

When I arrive at home, I am surprised to see the front door open and David's car in the driveway. I run in the door, calling to David, asking if he is alright.

As I run into the family room there is David, sitting in his usual chair, holding a finger to his lips. I look to the couch beside him, and there is Nicholas, fast asleep. Now, I know that Nicholas never lies down – nor lets anyone else lie down – during the day because in his world, people should only sleep at night.

My alarm bell goes off.

I look to David for an explanation.

"Well, it seems likely that he had a seizure at school this morning."

My heart freezes in my throat.

"I got a call at the office to come right away. They tried calling your cell phone but there was no answer."

Damn. I inwardly kick myself hard. I had forgotten to turn my cell phone back on after that lousy audition from hell!

I tune back in to what David is saying.

"It was during the morning national anthem. The teacher and Ms. Williams both reported that during the first verse of 'O Canada' he kind of fell back into his chair from his standing position. Then he stiffened and they said he had an 'otherworldly' look on his face for a minute or two. There may have been some twitching: Ms. Williams said his limbs were twitching; Mrs.

Ferguson didn't mention it. Then he 'came to' and was so tired he had to put his head on his arm on his desk to rest. I went and picked him up and he immediately fell asleep on the couch. He's been asleep for about an hour now.'

I drop my bag onto the floor and squirm out of my coat as I walk over to the couch. There he lies, like an angel, a look on his face like he is dreaming of meadows and butterflies.

I am highly distressed. And guilty. How could I have been so selfishly pursuing a few moments of shopping and eating and talking while this was happening to my son? And how could I not have had a twinge, an inkling, that something was wrong? What kind of a mother am I?

A seizure? He had never exhibited anything resembling a seizure before. I knew that seizure activity was not uncommon in children within the autistic spectrum, but we had not seen any evidence in the past nine years, and so we thought we were one of the lucky ones and had escaped that particular complication.

So did this episode brand him epileptic? Had he in fact been having petit mal seizures all along and we had just not been astute enough to detect them?

I look at David's worried face as he looks at his sleeping son.

"Have you called the doctor yet?" I ask.

"Yes, she can see us in an hour and a half."

I sit in the chair opposite David, both of us mutely staring at our son. Still the boy he was when he left for school this morning. Still in his shorts and tee shirt, still the same height and weight, eyelashes closed over the same blue eyes he had this morning. But different somehow. More fragile.

For the next hour we sit, pace and bite our nails waiting for him to wake up.

And he does.

I have to fight the urge to rush to him and embrace him and hold him close and assure him that everything will be OK. Even with so many years of practice, my maternal urges still kick in before I remember his extreme sensitivity to touch.

I stay where I am.

He opens his eyes and takes a moment to adjust to where he is. He sees me and David. We smile tenderly. We know to avoid startling him. I hide my concern, and speak softly.

"Hiya, Nic. How are you doing?"

He blinks a couple of times.

I give him a few more moments to wake up.

"So, do you remember that Dad came and got you from school this morning?"

"Yeah."

"Do you remember what happened at school?"

"Yes. I sat down in my chair. Then I got sleepy and put my head on my desk."

I look to David. So he doesn't remember anything about the seizure itself.

"Do you remember anything that happened before you sat down? Did you feel funny or unusual?"

"I'm not sure."

I explain to Nicholas that in twenty minutes we are going to see Dr. Ellis and tell her what happened at school this morning. And that she will want to look in his eyes and maybe touch him a bit. Will that be OK?

He gives a slight nod and then slumps back on the couch cushions. He is clearly exhausted.

"Can Dad feel your forehead to see if you are hot?"

"No."

We can leave that for the doctor I think.

I place a jacket over his shoulders to deflect any possibility of the doctor diagnosing unsuitable clothing as the cause for his seizure. We ease him into the car and drive to the clinic. He is still quite lethargic when we enter Dr. Ellis' office.

Nicholas refuses to sit up on her table, so she examines him while he sits in a chair between David and myself.

He tells her what he had told us about the incident. And we tell her what we had been told by the school staff.

When she finishes looking at him, she asks David to take him out to the waiting area so that she can talk to me. Nicholas doesn't even object or leave instructions like, "Don't say anything I don't like." Clearly not himself today.

She tells me that it does indeed sound like he experienced a seizure, particularly because of the classic symptom of being so tired afterwards. She tells me that she will make a referral with a neurologist for a complete work up.

Shaky and without any real answers to our many questions, we go home and watch our son. While he eats. While he sleeps. While he plays. Like hawks we are, never letting him out of our sights.

We cancel the next day's appointments and keep him home from school, the three of us watching and waiting for it to happen again.

Two days of waiting and watching, and we saw no signs of a repeat seizure.

But the phone rang. It was the neurologist's office, informing us of an appointment that had opened up due to a cancellation, and did we want to take it. I asked what the appointment would involve. The woman on the other end of the phone outlined the standard procedure: an hour prior to seeing the neurologist, Nicholas would undergo an electroencephalogram, known as an EEG, and then we would discuss the findings with the neurologist afterward.

I asked about the EEG. She calmly explained to me that my son would be required to lie still for an hour with twenty-seven electrodes attached to his head.

I laughed.

I asked if Dr. Dooley, the neurologist, had seen many patients in the autistic spectrum. She hesitated. I told her the reason I asked is that I couldn't imagine Nicholas being able to lie still for an hour, let alone having electrodes attached to his head. I simply couldn't see that happening without some kind of intervention. She went on to mention that it would be possible to administer a sedative prior to the procedure, but they preferred to avoid it, in case it interfered with the brain wave activity and compromised the reliability of the data.

I told her I would like to discuss this with my husband, and we signed off, agreeing on an appointment time day after next, but with the understanding that I would be in touch after talking to David and Nicholas to confirm.

I immediately called Nicholas' developmental pediatrician and told her of the incident and the appointment with the neurologist and asked her opinion. Knowing the procedure and knowing Nicholas, I figured she would be the best judge of how the two would go together.

The first thing she asked was if we had seen any further sign of seizure activity. I told her we hadn't.

I explained my concern about the EEG procedure. I wanted to avoid a high-stress situation for all involved unless it was absolutely necessary. With his anxiety levels and sensitivity to touch and sound, I had difficulty imagining this going well, even with all the preparation and social stories in the world. I reminded her of that time he had to have blood taken, and the four nurses that had to hold him down. I was also reluctant to spend taxpayers' money on a procedure that might have to be abandoned soon after it began.

She suggested then that we pass on the EEG for now, but keep our appointment with Dr. Dooley, so that he could examine Nicholas himself and ask the right questions, and give us some information.

I discussed all this with David. We took her advice, and a few days later the three of us meet with Dr. Dooley, a warm, charming Irishman who, on first impression, seems better suited to the entertainment industry than neural science.

He is a master at putting us all at our ease, and manages to examine Nicholas without Nicholas even realizing he was being examined.

Dr. Dooley asks us about family history of epilepsy. David mentions that he may have had a seizure once when he was less than two years of age.

Dr. Dooley asks us about possible environmental factors in the classroom that morning that might have served as a trigger for the seizure. We tell him, that as far as we know, everything was the same.

He asks what immediately preceded the episode. We tell him it happened during the national anthem.

"I have heard that colours or emotions can serve as triggers, but the national anthem?" David jokes.

I suggest that maybe someone was singing horribly off-key and that triggered Nicholas' seizure. Or maybe this was an early indication of possible anti-establishment leanings in our son.

Dr. Dooley makes some notes, probably about the questionable sanity of the patient's parents, then proceeds to give us some background information on epilepsy, using his computer to illustrate points and statistics.

He starts by saying that what has been described sounds like a classic seizure, that there was little chance of it being anything else. He tells us that a lot of children experience a seizure at some point during childhood, and that only about fifty percent of those go on to have more than one seizure, and therefore considered epileptic. He tells us that Nicholas may never experience another one, and in fact, the longer Nic goes without sign of another seizure, the greater his chances are of not having another one, and that unless we see evidence of another seizure, there is no real need to pursue the idea of an electroencephalogram at this time.

I sigh with relief.

He instructs us to send him back to school for the few remaining days of the school year, tells us to relax and resume our lives.

We leave, feeling hopeful that Nicholas' seizure was a one-off event, and determined to ask school staff to observe him closely during the last few days of school.

Particularly during the national anthem. Oh yes, we'll be standing on guard for thee.

Summer Vacation

Today's Agenda

I came across this, taped to the kitchen wall, one sunny summer's morning when I was preparing to make tea.

Nicholas told me it was his agenda for the day.

8:50 Pets and Games ☐
8:57 Yard Sales ☐
9:00 Wordo ☐
9:17 Downstairs ☐
9:30 Hang Posters Up ☐
10:00 Just stuff ☐
10:30 workroom ☐
10:50 Nothing ☐

11:00 Etc ☐
11:14 Everything else ☐
11:30 Do things ☐
12:00 Solitaire ☐
12:50 Whatever ☐
12:54 Anywhere ☐

1:00 Work on
    the Computer ☐
1:30 Do a trick with silver ☐
2:00 Hangman ☐
2:30 Done ☐

Sounds like a pretty terrific summer day to me.

August 18th: David's Birthday

The Case of the Lost Parents (or These Lost Parents Are a Case)

Investigative Report

Detective: Lorne Ranger, Private Investigator

Date: August 18th, 2001

Time: ten o'clock in the evening.

Place: the Overton home

Crime: parental self-neglect

I received the call shortly after nine p.m. the evening of the eighteenth. The voice on the other end of the phone claimed to be the Overtons' neighbour. She was near hysterical, worried that the Overtons, David and Jennifer, had not arrived as expected at the neighbour's home.

I told her to calm down and tell me what she knew. Just the facts.

She took a deep breath. She explained that August 18th was David Overton's birthday, and to celebrate, the two couples had planned to meet for a glass of champagne at the neighbour's house at eight-thirty that evening. When the Overtons didn't show, the neighbours waited twenty minutes, and then walked over to the Overton house and knocked on the front and back doors, getting no response. They rang the doorbell repeatedly, shouted for the Overtons to open the door. No response. They noted that a light was on in the house and the car was in the driveway. They returned to their home and tried calling the Overton house. Each of the five times they called, the Overton phone would ring, the receiver would be picked up, then immediately hung up.

They felt as though the Overtons might be in trouble. They called me.

Further questions revealed that the Overton's only son, eight-year-old Nicholas Overton, was away on an overnight camping trip.

The Crime Scene

I arrived at the Overton house at approximately nine forty-five p.m. I approached the front door and knocked hard, skinning my knuckles in the process. No response. Next I rang the doorbell. Long and hard. It left the tip of my index finger a little tender. Still no response. I walked around the dark house to the back. I noted that a light was on in one of the upstairs rooms. I walked past the sleeping dog to the back door. It was locked, but a light push on the door opened it. Obviously not latched properly. If there was an assailant in the house, perhaps this was the point of entry.

I made a mental note that the Overtons should get a new latch. And a new dog.

I made my way into the moonlit kitchen, my hand on my holster. I listened. Hearing nothing, I began to make my way slowly and quietly through the downstairs rooms. Nothing. No sign of a break-in or anything untoward, although I did notice an open canister of Pringles potato chips on the coffee table in the family room. I returned the lid to the canister. It's a crime to let those things get stale.

Satisfied that all was in order downstairs, I began my slow ascent up the stairs. From the stairs I determined that the light that I saw from the backyard was in fact coming from the master bedroom.

The only sound emanating from the master bedroom was a low mumbling, like the sound of someone tied up and trying to cry out for help.

Fearing the worst, I pulled my revolver from its holster and held it poised for action. Sliding against the hallway wall, I slowly and quietly made my way toward the bedroom. I snapped open the door and pointed my revolver, hoping to surprise the perpetrator.

Once my eyes adjusted to the light in the bedroom, I saw the Overtons. On the bed. On top of the covers. Fully clothed in formal clothing. Wide awake.

They let out a small shriek.

By the light of the bedside lamp, I discerned that the Overtons were not tied up, nor was there any evidence of foul play. They were just lying on the bed, looking lost.

But it was clear some form of crime had taken place here. The bedroom was in severe disorder. The Overtons were surrounded by telephones of all sizes and descriptions. Cellular phones lay beside them on the bed, and wireless phones were placed on the floor beside the bed. Touchtone phones had apparently been dragged into the bedroom from other rooms. There was even an old dial phone on the nightstand.

The room was also strewn with boys' clothing: shorts, long pants, socks. The Overtons were clutching a pair of boys' pajamas, rubbing their cheeks with the soft, hockey-logoed fabric.

The floor of the bedroom was littered with toys: Nintendo°, and various hand-held electronic games, including Math Quiz, Wheel of Fortune, and Hangman. I also noted several books on the subjects of botany and wild birdlife.

After taking in the scene, I checked behind drapes and in the closet. Whoever had been there holding the couple hostage had fled.

I holstered my weapon and cautiously approached the Overtons on the bed. I assured them that they were all right. I identified myself.

Upon approach, I noted a wild-eyed look on both their frantic faces. When I asked them what had happened here, Mrs. Overton only muttered over and over, "I wonder how he's doing."

These people needed help. Whatever had transpired in that room had left them traumatized. They were lost. Real lost.

I needed to find out what had happened.

I sat on the edge of the bed and told them that I was going to take them downstairs and talk about the incident, difficult as that might be, and that I would do everything in my power to find the person responsible for their distress.

Still mumbling and shaky, the Overtons accompanied me downstairs to the family room. They sat on the couch, I took the fireside chair.

I poured glasses of water for the victims. I opened the canister of Pringles, popped a short stack into my mouth, and began my questioning. I asked them to start at the beginning, take their time, and tell me everything that had happened.

The Interrogation

They began by telling me what the neighbour had told me: that today was a special day because it was Mr. Overton's birthday. It was also special because it was the first time that their only son, known as Nicholas, a.k.a. Nic, a.k.a. Sweetie, was leaving to go on his first ever overnight camping trip with the special needs day camp he had been attending the past few weeks.

Mr. and Mrs. Overton were looking forward to their first night alone in eight years.

They told me they had planned everything very carefully. The sleeping bag had been aired out, the overnight bag packed with everything he could want or need on his trip. The itinerary had been reviewed and discussed.

It had been agreed all around that this overnight adventure would be good for the whole
family.

At least that's what the innocent Overtons
thought.

The morning of the crime started just as
planned. Mr. And Mrs. Overton drove their son
to the usual drop-off place for the day camp.
They handed the counselors the sleeping bag,
the suitcase, his pillow, and a sheet of paper
titled "Nic Notes" which contained information about his nighttime routine and food
preferences. It also included several contact
phone numbers where the parents could be
reached should there be a problem or a question
of any kind.

The counselors assured the Overtons that
everything would be fine. The Overton boy
climbed into the van and took his usual seat.

The Overtons tried to believe that this was
a positive independent step for their son, and
said goodbyes and waved nervously as the camp
van pulled out of the parking lot.

Mr. Overton stated that once the van was out
of sight, the Overtons began their
thirty-two-hour vacation with a high five.
They jumped into their car, and, feeling like
carefree teenagers, they turned up the radio
and drove away, responsibility free.

They first stopped at a diner and ordered a
big, cholesterol-laden breakfast.

Note: in follow-up investigation, a waitress
at the diner did indeed remember the Overtons,

and observed them laughing and playing footsie under the table while they ate.

Their next stop was the liquor store, where a medium-priced bottle of champagne was purchased.

They then drove to the university to clear some paperwork off Mr. Overton's desk, and to enjoy a birthday cup of coffee with colleagues.

They claimed that at approximately eleven a.m. they were seen by many witnesses strolling in the Public Gardens, feeding the ducks and chatting animatedly on a park bench. Mr. Overton reported that he and Mrs. Overton had chased each other, and at one point, he had tackled Mrs. Overton and tickled her to the ground, where they lay for several minutes giggling like children.

Note: This was later confirmed by a member of the park staff, who had certainly remembered the Overtons; and who was so appalled at their behaviour that he was on the verge of calling the park commissionaire when the Overton couple got up, brushed the grass off their knees, and made their way back to their car.

A light bistro lunch was eaten at a sidewalk café. This was confirmed by the parking ticket the Overtons showed me.

Next in their vacation plan was a lazy walk along the waterfront, and a shared ice cream cone.

The only indication that these two people had any cares in the world at all was the occasional glance at the cellular phone that Mrs. Overton carried in her bag.

At approximately three-thirty p.m. the Overtons claimed to have returned home.

The Confession

Their plan was to have a half-hour nap, followed by dressing for dinner, and then to the casino, and then to dinner, to be followed by a visit to the neighbours for a celebratory glass of champagne.

The casino. I love the casino.

Mr. Overton put the champagne on ice before their nap.

They woke from what they described as their refreshing nap at exactly four-thirty. This was confirmed by the setting of the alarm clock on the bedside table.

And that's when the Overtons claimed things began to fall apart.

I handed Mrs. Overton a tissue as she explained that when they woke from their nap, it was four-thirty, and that was usually when their son was home from camp. But that day he wasn't there because of the overnight camp.

They had tried to continue with their plans and dress for dinner, but they couldn't seem to concentrate. Mr. Overton put on his suit jacket inside out, and Mrs. Overton caught herself wearing brown shoes with a black dress.

They sat down on the bed and stared at each other. They looked at the bedside clock. Five o'clock.

They reminded themselves of the romantic child-free night they had ahead of them, and, after some alterations to what they were wearing, they left the bedroom and headed toward the stairs.

But they never made it down the stairs.

Mrs. Overton, try as she might to walk down the stairs, kept swerving toward their son's bedroom, walking into it and smelling the clothes in his closet. Meanwhile, Mr. Overton found himself at the computer and putting in the Wheel of Fortune compact disc, and wiping a nostalgic tear from his eye.

Mr. Overton finally tore himself away from his son's favourite game and went to find Mrs. Overton. He found her in their son's room, curled up on his bed, hugging his pillow and staring out the window repeating, "I wonder what he's doing now. I hope he's OK without us."

From there they abandoned their plans and retreated to the bedroom, awaiting what they felt was the inevitable call from the camp asking them to come and pick up their son because he was so desperately homesick.

When I told them that their neighbours had called me, concerned about their well-being, and asked why the phone was hung up every time the neighbours tried to call, the pathetic Overtons lifted their sorry heads and said that when they saw the neighbour's number on the call display, they immediately hung up so as not to tie up the lines for when the camp called.

I gently directed their attention to the clock in the family room. The time was ten-thirty.

I suggested that their son was probably fast asleep by now, and that they might want to consider getting ready for bed themselves.

The crime here was obvious. These parents had forgotten how to be carefree after four o'clock in the afternoon.

I helped them back upstairs and turned on some lights for them to get ready for bed. I tucked them in, sang them a lullaby, turned out the lights when I was sure they were asleep, left the house, and locked the back door behind me. Properly this time. The dog let out a big snore as I walked over her.

I used my cellular phone to call the neighbours and tell them the sad story and assure them that the Overtons were safe and were going to be all right at approximately four o'clock the following day when their son was due to return from his overnight camp.

I encouraged them to check on them the next day to make sure they ate a little and drank plenty of fluids.

The neighbours were grateful to me. All in a day's work I told them.

I shook my head as I headed back to my car.

I checked my watch as I drove away. Eleven o'clock. The casino would be open for another hour.

The First Monday in September: Labour Day

The Five Stages

On a cold, damp autumn day in 1996, our life took a major turn.

Our family experienced a death.

Not the death of a person. Or the loss of a family pet. But the death of a hope; the death of a future that we had envisioned.

Our son was diagnosed with autism. And our world was turned upside down.

As with the sudden passing of someone close to you, or a major trauma of some kind, where you must face a future entirely different from the one you had anticipated, a grieving process must take place. Grieving the loss, the death, of something.

In our case, and only with hindsight, have we come to realize that part of the process has been grieving the death of the life we thought we had, while at the same time adjusting to, and accepting, the life we do have.

Having to deal with grief and nurture our son simultaneously has at times been very difficult.

Elizabeth Kübler-Ross provides a framework for the five stages of grief: Denial; Bargaining; Anger/Resentment; Depression; and finally, Acceptance.

Here's how we experienced those five stages.

Denial

By the time we sought out and received Nicholas' first diagnosis, we were already well through this stage, having been reluctant to confront the signs of his autism for the previous eighteen months or so.

But when we saw the television program about autism and saw our son in those autistic children's eyes, we could no longer deny our son's developmental differences. That day we found ourselves bewildered and lost in the world of Autism.

Bargaining

Our first diagnosis was received on the eve of Nicholas' fourth birthday. The private psychologist that we had hired to assess our son concluded that our son was PDDNOS. Pervasive Developmental Disorder, Not Otherwise Specified. Well that made it so much clearer. Not. To our stunned and empty faces she began to explain in clinical-speak the basis for the diagnosis: his deficiencies in the areas of social interaction, his atypical communication skills, and his behavioural issues, the combination of which added up to his diagnosis within the autism spectrum.

We knew nothing about autism. Sure, we had seen the movie *Rainman* and had been fascinated by the story and the character, but we had watched it when Nicholas was just an infant, long before there was any inkling that the disorder depicted in the film would have such enormous impact on our lives. To us it was entertainment, not relevant to us in any way.

We left her office with our same but now different son. I remember standing on the front steps of the clinic, David and I on either side of Nicholas, each of us holding one of his little hands, and looking over Nicholas' head at one another, not moving, not knowing what to do or where to go. Looking down at our son.

Looking at the piece of paper in my hand. Then looking down again at our son.

Bargain #1: If we ignore it, maybe it will go away, and everything will be all right.

The rest of that day we just sat in the living room without talking. We watched Nicholas at play with different eyes. Too overwhelmed to even cry. Silently sifting the psychologist's words, reading the diagnosis over and over. At an absolute loss as to what our son was and what he needed.

We hoped that if we just sat there and waited patiently, it would all go away. We sat, waiting, for days.

Bargain #2: If knowledge is power, maybe knowledge will make everything all right.

Realizing that sitting on the couch wasn't giving the desired results, I decided that knowledge might give us power and make everything all right.

I went to the library and took out a lot of books. I randomly chose whatever books about autism I could find – I had no recommended reading list. I took out books written by clinicians, books written by parents who had brought their children back from the clutches of autism, books written by people with autism. I brought the books home and plopped them on the living room floor beside the sofa and started to read, desperate to find my son within the pages, and get answers as to how to help him.

I became consumed with learning all I could about Autism/PDD.

Then our name came to the top of the waiting list at the Developmental Clinic at the children's hospital. In addition to our private diagnosis, we were anxious to get what we hoped would be a more specific, definitive diagnosis from the autism experts at the hospital.

After the questionnaires and parental observation forms had been filled out, the family history questions answered, and the battery of tests performed on Nicholas, we got our answer: Autistic Spectrum Disorder. To us this diagnosis was just as vague as his first diagnosis of PDDNOS. It was explained to us that currently all children found to belong within the spectrum were receiving the more general diagnosis of Autism Spectrum Disorder. We weren't told why. But whatever the reason, this label didn't indicate to us his level of functioning, his potential, or how his future might look. In retrospect, perhaps the hospital's policy was a way of ensuring educational assistance for as many spectrum children as possible when it came time for them to go to school.

But school was a while away. What were we to do now?

She explained that although autism has no known cause and no cure, there are treatments, and that early intervention is essential. She recommended that we seek out the service of a qualified speech and language therapist, and make an appointment with the Developmental Clinic's developmental pediatrician. She also suggested we join the Autism Society of Mainland Nova Scotia.

We did all three.

Bargain # 3: If we get organized, everything will be all right.

I made an appointment with the public Speech and Language Clinic. I was told there was a six-month waiting list. And there was a substantial waiting list to see the developmental pediatrician.

The waiting list for the developmental pediatrician was one that we could do nothing about. But we refused to wait out the long list for public speech and language services.

David and I discussed our financial situation and what we could afford to do. We realized that I would have to turn down work for the next little while until we got Nicholas' needs sorted out.

We hired the private services of a practical and highly committed speech and language therapist named Betsy Allard. Our first consultation with her was at our home, as she wanted to assess him in his own environment.

She conducted some preliminary reading and vocabulary tests on Nicholas and was delighted to hear him read so well. She was also interested to hear some of the strategies we had already been employing since his diagnosis. For instance, when I realized that Nicholas was a visual learner, I decided to use his reading skills to teach him things. So when Nicholas met my request to get dressed with an innocent blank stare, I got out paper and pencil and made a list of steps involved in getting dressed.

1.   Take off pajamas.

2.   Go to dresser drawer #1 and get clean underwear.

3.   Put on underwear with the 'Y' at the front.

4.   Get clean shirt from dresser drawer #2.

5.   Put on shirt with the tag at the back.

6.   Get clean pants from dresser drawer #3.

7.   Put on pants with the zipper at the front.

8.   Get clean socks from drawer #4.

9.   Put on socks.

We read the list together. After reading it once, I covered it up and asked him what it had said. He recited the list exactly. I left the list on the wall beside his dresser for his reference. I knew we were on to something. No more blank stares when I asked him to get dressed.

I also showed Betsy the kitchen cupboards and dining room walls plastered with labeled verb pictures cards. I had spent many evenings cutting out pictures from magazines and pasting and labeling them on cards. There were pictures of people *dancing*; children *reaching*; adults *cooking*. The easel in the living room that usually held Grandpa's painting of Indian Cove was now in use as a stand for the posterboard charts I made for Nicholas. I charted and categorized different animals and where they lived, what they ate, and descriptors. This seemed to organize the information into manageable units for him. And just about every object in the house had a name tag on it.

Betsy and I talked at that first house meeting about his speech delay, echolalia (repeating words said to him), his self-taught reading, his unreliability with pronoun usage, and his uneven skill development. She suggested pinning a piece of paper with the word 'I' to the front of his shirt, and referring him to it when he referred to himself. Brilliant! Finally we were cluing in to his learning style and using it to teach him.

Bargain #4: If I become his trainer, then everything will be all right.

During these weeks and months after his fourth birthday, he was still attending preschool part time. He attended the church basement neighbourhood nursery school two mornings a week, as well as the Child Study Centre, which was attached to the university where I was finishing my part-time contract, teaching two mornings a week.

David and I decided that to help him and the staff at the nursery school, I would accompany him there the two mornings a week. That was very tough for me. It was so painful to see him in the midst of other children, clearly not one of them, and them baffled by him. I remember having to hold him on my lap and insisting he do crafts, at the same time trying to write out lists and instructions for him. But he would often become noncompliant and aggressive. Getting his jacket and boots on to go home at the end of one particularly difficult morning at nursery school, I overheard one sweet little girl saying to her mother, "I think they adopted Nicholas, Mommy." I barely made it to the car before the tears gushed out of me. Did she and her family and probably all the other four-year-olds and their families spend time coming up with explanations as to how this child could be of these parents? Was it so inconceivable to that four-year-old's mind that Nicholas be born of me and David?

Needless to say, my skin was pretty thin in those early days.

Next, we had our appointment with the developmental pediatrician at the children's hospital. Dr. Hawkins was warm, soft-spoken and confident.

She discussed with us the diagnosis received from the hospital's autism expert. We talked about his current educational setting. Rather than having him enrolled in two different preschool programs – one in the neighbourhood and another at the university, she suggested that we choose one place for him in order to offer more routine and stability, and to avoid confusion for him. She also suggested that if we could afford it, we should increase his time there to five mornings a week.

We also talked about his sensory sensitivities: hearing and touch. We decided to get his hearing tested to check if his actual hearing was OK. She knew that the occupational therapist we were on a waiting list to see would have strategies for dealing with his vestibular (balance and movement) and sensory issues. She cautioned against forcing him into physical activity that he wasn't comfortable with.

We talked about treatment plans. She gave me reading lists and resource information on the major schools of thought regarding treatment for children with autism. She gave me the address of the Geneva Center in Toronto. She neither endorsed nor belittled any of the various approaches to autism, but did warn us to carefully research and adopt an approach that would suit our family's emotional and financial situation. She warned us to proceed with caution, reminded us there was no cure, and praised us for the wonderful strategies we had come up with already.

We left her office without our hoped-for referral to an Autism Centre that would take us by the hand, assess all our needs, co-ordinate and implement the treatment(s) that might be best for Nicholas, answer all our questions, and anticipate all of our needs. But that centre existed only in our fevered imaginations.

If our son had cancer instead of autism, that centre might exist.

That night I had a repeat of a dream that I had when I was pregnant: I had just purchased a beautiful new bassinet with carrying handles. I wanted desperately to try it out. So I reached up inside my body and pulled the baby out of me and placed it in the bassinet, and walked around the living room, admiring how nice the baby looked in the bassinet. But when I looked more closely at the baby, I noticed that its legs and arms were not fully developed – they resembled stumps rather than limbs. Not only that but they had hooves at the ends. Panicked that I had plucked the baby out of my body before it was finished developing, I tried desperately to push it back in, so that it could finish growing. I was frantically trying to push it back inside me when I woke up.

That dream had shaken me quite a bit when I was eight months pregnant. David and I just put it down to natural prenatal anxiety, and maybe watching *Rosemary's Baby* once too often. But having the same dream again when he was four, and just having been diagnosed with autism, was eerie.

Since it was becoming increasingly apparent that there was no place in Canada to get the help we needed for our son, I began investigating American institutes and continued my reading and research. I attended conferences.

One of the local conferences I attended featured a noted Halifax psychiatrist. After his presentation, I approached him and asked him to see our son. He agreed. He met with Nicholas and David and me. He asked Nicholas and us questions. I don't know why, but I remember Nicholas interrupting the psychiatrist's conversation with us, demanding I tie his right brown shoe.

The psychiatrist's diagnosis: mild autism, possible Asperger Syndrome.

So now we had three different diagnoses for our son.

It wasn't until years later that I suspected that, when it comes to autism, the diagnosis one receives depends a bit on the person one asks.

What we did know was that our son was high-functioning autistic: he was verbal, bright, and needed a lot of help. And it looked like no one was offering to give it to him… It was up to us.

Bargain #5: If we investigate other factors, maybe it won't turn out to be autism, and everything will be all right.

All the literature had stressed that early intervention was crucial to stand a chance of achieving reasonable functioning levels. Guilty about our months of denial and angry at long waiting lists for services, we overcompensated for our ignorance, and launched into action like whirling dervishes, not sure where we were going.

First, we had him tested for food and chemical sensitivities. What came out of that test was that he had unusually high levels of aluminum in his body. Aluminum? I know that aluminum is all around us, but how did one get an overdose of aluminum? We were told that vaccinations have high levels of aluminum. We had already heard concerns about immature nervous systems being bombarded with vaccinations that may be toxic. Right. No more vaccinations for him. What about penicillin? He had taken one course of penicillin during his one and only ear infection at fourteen months of age. I had read about possible links between overuse of penicillin and autism. Right. No more penicillin for Nicholas, unless it was absolutely necessary.

Since traditional medicine offered no help for our son, we decided to explore one non-traditional therapy. We chose homeopathy. It is not toxic to the body and carries no side-effects or risks. And it has been safely practised for thousands of years. Nicholas began a course of treatment that would span two homeopathic practitioners and five years.

While we were busy explicitly and visually teaching what we felt he needed to know in terms of general knowledge and self-help skills, we contacted community services to set up structured play dates to work on his social skills.

They ended up being disastrous, as the play environment was not structured to accommodate autistic kids, and it was so over-stimulating that Nicholas would immediately retreat deep inside the large play tent when we arrived and refuse to emerge until promised that we would leave. Not a lot of social or play skills can be learned at the back of a tent. Well, not for a four-year-old anyway.

We had his hearing tested. It was within normal range. We bought a set of noise reduction headphones like the ones worn by construction workers. He began to wear them when in noisy or auditorily confusing environments, like preschool.

Bargain #6: If we throw a lot of money at the problem, everything will be all right.

Preschool. Unfortunately, we were realizing that the philosophy of the preschool at the university was contrary to what we were learning our son needed. It was a university early childhood education learning centre, and the emphasis was on open play and child-led activities. Well, when allowed, all my child wanted to do was sing Broadway show tunes and spell words. They were at a loss. There were safety issues with other children. He was clearly overstimulated by all the levels of noise and the lack of structure.

At one of the parent–teacher meetings, we met another couple whose son was in the process of being diagnosed. We began talking about the need for treatment and how the current educational setting at the preschool was not meeting our children's needs. But where else was there?

It turned out that there was yet another set of parents in the preschool in the same process of diagnosis of their son within the spectrum, and they were facing the same questions. The three couples began a series of brainstorming sessions aimed at trying to find solutions to accommodate their sons' needs. Together, and at a cost of approximately twenty thousand dollars each, we created the first ever Pilot Project for Preschoolers with Autism in this province. The three target children were the same age, all boys, each at differing points along the spectrum.

The process went something like this: We spoke to the director of the preschool about the feasibility of setting up a special program for these three families. We asked if a quieter room in the preschool could be set aside for the program we proposed. Ideally, we would like a room sound-proofed. We proposed to adopt the programming of a major New England autism treatment institute from the United States. We would fly the New England experts up to Nova Scotia and pay for them to assess our children and set up individual programs for each of them. We would also pay them to train the local staff we were planning to hire to work one-on-one with our children. We would also hire a private speech and language therapist to work with the children and contribute to their programming. The programs for these three children would consist of intensive, highly structured one-on-one training, inter-spersed with structured group activities with the typical children in the preschool, like circle and story times.

We didn't have time to wait for government funding of any kind. We thought that we would pay for it the first year, and then the government would see what a great idea it was and of course they would financially support the program in future years. We three couples borrowed money from our families, took out loans, and second-mortgaged our homes.

The decision to employ a Lovaas-based treatment institute from New England was not a simple one, and I had my reserva-tions about it from the start.

In retrospect, I do agree with the premise of Applied Behav-ioural Analysis: teaching skills by breaking tasks down into small units. Nicholas did need to be taught everything explicitly. But where Lovass and I differ is the teaching methodology. I realize many children have benefited from this approach; but in my mind, Nicholas did not need the strict rote, repetitive, constantly rein-forced approach to learning skills. Yes, he needed to be taught, but he learned quickly. To me, the Lovaas approach smacked a bit of 'training a seal to jump for treats' that I found distasteful and diffi-cult to come to terms with. I remember hearing someone talking about the benefits of Lovaas, and how so many children had become indistinguable from their peers in a 'well, if it walks like a duck and sounds like a duck it must be a duck' analogy. It was like they wanted to change their children. Make them normal. Well, my son is who he is, and his uniqueness is not a defect; nothing is wrong with him, rather there is something different about him. We didn't want to 'fix' him, to make him like everyone else. Our goal was and always has been to give him strategies to cope with the world that he must find very baffling.

In addition, I was confused that the Lovaas practitioners seemed unsympathetic to his sensory sensitivities and central auditory processing difficulties. When I described his auditory sensitivity and processing difficulties, and his need to wear his earphones in particular environments, they replied, "Oh, he won't be wearing those any more. He needs to learn to function in a noisy environment without those." Well, the question that I wish I could have articulated at that time was, "Yes, but how can he learn anything when bombarded with so much stimulation?"

What did I know? I didn't have enough perspective, experience, or research then to listen to my own heart and state what I felt was right for my son.

Needless to say, the program did have many benefits for Nicholas. The one-on-one approach to instruction in a quiet setting really helped him to learn things, and the employment of his hyperlexic learning style (early reading skills) allowed him to progress even more quickly. And he was certainly table ready in time to start school.

During this year and a half of the pilot program, I enrolled him in private music lessons at the Atlantic Provinces Special Education Authority. Although most of their students were visually or hearing impaired, I wanted to cultivate his keen musical sense, love of rhythm, seemingly perfect pitch, and extraordinary memory for music. In fact, we had come to make up songs often to teach him things or get his attention. So I thought it was the perfect extracurricular activity.

Non-compliance on Nicholas' part combined with inexperience with autism on the instructor's part made the sessions trying. But his recital was spectacular. Our little four-year-old son, smartly dressed in white shirt, bow tie, and black trousers, with his mop of mussed hair, sitting at a piano plunking out the song *Lollipop, Lollipop*. At the end he hopped down from the piano bench and bowed. He covered his ears when the audience applauded. We were ecstatic with his performance.

I showed the videotape to the Lovaas people when they next came to Halifax to monitor the boys' preschool programs, and they were amazed at what they saw. "How did you get him to do that?" they asked, their mouths hanging open. "I wrote out what would happen." I replied. They said nothing.

Anger and resentment

We had been launched into autism orbit, and after circling for eighteen months, I began to tire. I was active in the Autism Society, and I had joined with the energy and commitment of the newly diagnosed, determined to change the way autism was perceived and treated.

But autism is a particularly draining disorder to live with, and it was wearing me down. It was very difficult not taking any time to grieve our situation because we were so desperately busy trying to help our child. Normal emotions and necessary reactions were forced underground where they silently began to swell. And one day at the mall I saw the tip of a very large ugly emotional iceberg come to the surface.

It was nine-thirty in the morning and I had just dropped Nicholas off at his pilot project preschool program for his eight hours of intensive instruction. I was sitting on a bench in the mall waiting for a store to open, when I saw a couple of young women with their toddlers approaching. The moms were talking to each other, laughing and smoking. Their children were eating chips and drinking colas. The toddlers were noisy and boisterous, and curiously exploring everything. The mothers would pause in their conversation long enough to yell at their children, and then resume smoking and gossiping. Moments later their adoring children would run up and hug their indifferent mothers.

The anger welled up in me. How dare they. How dare they take for granted their children's health and affection! What I wouldn't give to have a spontaneous hug from my child! I feed my child healthy food! I give him attention! I don't smoke!!!! Why does my child have autism? I continued to watch with growing resentment as the mothers slapped away their children's hands and harshly told them to go away. Hot tears began to flow. The tip of that anger was so hot and pointy that I had to abandon my shopping plans and drive home, unsuccessfully attempting to hold back the hot flood of tears that scared me.

Time was up. I could no longer avoid that growing iceberg. It was time to finally acknowledge my anger and resentment.

I made arrangements to take some time and drive to Peggy's Cove. I deflected all questions as to where I was going and why. I needed to be far from home to sit quietly and measure the size of this iceberg. I had to talk to myself about it before I could talk to anyone else about it.

I was not looking forward to opening this particular door of my psyche. I didn't want revealed, even to myself, the nasty ugly thoughts and feelings I harboured. The words of my mother had been going through my mind the past few days. When Nicholas was diagnosed, I had confessed to her, in a flood of tears, that I didn't know why this was happening; that I felt as if this was personal, a result of something I had done. She had told me that soon I would see that I wasn't being punished. But rather that I had been chosen for this challenge. I knew she was right. And I tried to feel that way. But the last little while, if I was to be honest with myself, I didn't feel that way. Sorry, Mom. Sorry, God. I was mad.

I stuffed my pockets with Kleenex tissues and put on my sneakers. I walked out the door, leaving David in charge. I had to go to Peggy's Cove. I had to walk the rocks and listen to the crash of the ocean.

Walking the bleak rocks under the threatening sky, I admitted to myself that I was having trouble dealing with my situation. I wasn't at peace with it the way David seemed to be. David seemed to be taking everything in his stride. He loves his son uncondition- ally. I love him too. But these days I don't always like him. I resent him. I resent him for coming into my life and turning it upside down. I resent him for putting a strain on our marriage. I resent the brakes I've had to put on my career — such as it was — to put every ounce of my energy into his well-being. I resent friends who have children as part of their life, while my child consumes my life. I resent the time I spend preparing school work, home work, life work, social scripts and stories for him. I resent having to be the chair of the Nicholas Overton Board of Directors, the co-ordinator, executive director and operations manager of the Nicholas Overton Foundation. I resent the fact that if my child had virtually any other medical condition, treatment would be forth- coming and he would receive all the services he required, and I wouldn't have to bear the burden of organizing his treatment and delivering a fair amount of it.

I yelled at the seagulls to shut up.

I sat and cried, feeling both ashamed and relieved to admit these feelings.

Before I left the cove, I walked over to the lighthouse and stared at its flashing beacon.

I vowed to work toward more balance in my life. I realized that it was just as important to Nicholas' welfare that his mom not crumble. I would be no good to him if I was not good to myself. I couldn't be a perfect mom. But I could try to be a happier mom.

I had to take time to do things not related to autism. The first step would be that I would withdraw from the Autism Society. Instead of spending our one night out a month together in a room with a group of other frazzled and desperate parents talking about autism, David and I should spend that evening as far away from autism as we could. Dinner. Dancing. Maybe a movie.

This would be the first step in reclaiming a life of sorts, and minimizing the growth of that iceberg of resentment. I promised myself to keep that iceberg in my sights in order to avoid hitting it again.

I felt ready to return home. I apologized to the seagulls and offered them some old sunflower seeds I found in my pocket. I got in the car and drove the fifteen minutes home with the windows down and the radio turned up.

Depression

Then came the time for Nicholas to go to school. Real school. David and I had done a lot of research on possible schools for him. We considered private schools with their low teacher/student ratios. But many of them would not consider accepting a child with behaviour problems. We considered home schooling. For about five minutes. Much as I love and am devoted to my son and his education, I knew deep in my heart that for me to home school him would be disastrous for both of us. Besides, I was working towards more balance, not more work. Hiring a teacher to teach him privately at home was out of the question financially. There was a new private school for attention-deficit children opening up in the city and we seriously considered that option. After all, the teacher/student ratio was one to three, and the rooms were small and quiet, and computers played a large role in the curriculum. In the end though, we decided against it, as Nicholas' skills and challenges were different from the majority of the school population, and we were concerned he would find the environment unsuitable.

That left public school. The public school in our neighbourhood is small with a population of a few hundred students. That was good. We felt it important that he attend school with neighbourhood kids. Although the school had never had a student with autism attend prior to Nicholas, the principal seemed genuinely supportive of Nicholas' needs, to the point of restructuring a washroom off the primary classroom into a quiet room for Nicholas to retreat to when overstimulated, and needing a break from the regular classroom. There was a resource teacher who would oversee Nicholas' Individual Program Plan, or IPP. He would have a full-time Educational Program Assistant (EPA) to adapt the curriculum to suit his learning style. He would have access to psychological and speech and language services.

We decided to send him to public school.

Once our decision was made, and we made it in plenty of time to prepare the school for his arrival, the staff at the school began their research by observing Nicholas and his trainers at the Pilot Project. While David and I made it clear that we did not expect the public school to adopt an Applied Behavioural Analysis approach for our son, we did stress the importance of adhering to some of the strategies employed by the Pilot Project staff. And when Nicholas' EPA was chosen, we paid for her to observe and talk to the Pilot Project team about Nicholas before he started school.

Books were loaned to the school staff, invitations to conferences were extended, meetings between the school psychologists and speech therapists were arranged with our private professionals to exchange ideas and smooth the transition from their care to the school's care. We wrote a lot of social stories about starting school and what he might encounter and how he could deal with things. We really wanted to do everything possible to set the stage for success.

Months and months of preparation before the first day of school.

The school offered their own great ideas to ease him into the routine. The week before school began, they dropped off photographs of all the teachers and staff to our house so that he would be prepared visually. We took a private tour of his classroom, and showed him where he would sit, and visited his 'little room' as we called it, with his favourite beanbag chair for when he needed a break. The driver of the special bus that Nicholas would ride came by to introduce himself and the bus to us. Nicholas got to go on it and try out his seat and practise fastening the seatbelt days before he was to get on it to go to school.

The actual first day of school we kept him home, as we knew it would be absolute chaos there. Instead, I went to the school and talked to the kids about Nicholas and read to them a story about Nicholas that I had written. I answered their questions about autism. I wanted them to know that Nicholas was autistic in order for them to understand his behaviour to some extent. I also wanted to avoid teasing in the playground, and I figured that they would be more likely to accept him and help him in the playground if they knew there was a reason for why he is the way he is. I also wanted to empower them. I told them that they could help Nicholas to learn to be a friend, and help him to learn by not getting too close to him and not being too loud around Nicholas, as that really hurt his ears. I showed them his earphones. The teacher had managed to get a box full of headphones used with a computer program and she had offered a pair to each of the children to try them on and find out how much quieter the room was when wearing headphones. We made a lot of noise without the headphones on, and then with them on. This was great, as it gave them a concrete appreciation for what he experienced.

The children and teacher seemed to appreciate me coming in, and I waved goodbye to their smiling nervous faces.

The next day was his first day of school. I was awake very early, pacing the house waiting for David and Nicholas to wake up. I tried very hard to hide my nerves as we prepared for school and filled his school bag with all that he would need and want: lunch, snacks, social stories, and toys.

The bus arrived. We walked out the door and walked him to the bus. I reminded him to say good morning to everyone. The bus driver, tuning in to my tight jaw and stiff stride, gave me warm smile and a reassuring wink. I told him to tell the school that I would be home all day should the school need me for anything. I boarded the bus and watched Nicholas as he took his seat, did up his seatbelt, and stared out the window.

The bus driver had to practically shove me off the bus, and David and I stood at the end of our driveway waving wildly as the bus pulled away. "Have a great day," I whispered, and blew the bus a kiss.

I stood there for ten minutes after the bus had gone.

So this was it? All that work, for this? To just hand him over to strangers who, despite all their interest and commitment and education, don't really have a clue as to what makes my son tick? Maybe we should have home-schooled him. Maybe we should have intensified his preschool time to fifty hours a week. Maybe we could have done more to prepare him. And them for him.

A wave of depression came over me. I recognized it as the same feeling I had the day after a show opened. All that hype to get to opening night, and then the slump.

I knew I had better keep busy.

I went into the house. I tried to take my mind off worrying how he was doing by throwing myself into some serious closet organizing. Didn't work. I tried calling a few friends to chat, but their lines were either busy or I got answering machines. So I ended up sitting in the living room, staring out the window wondering how and what he was doing, and how they were coping with him.

I despaired. What if all we had done was not enough and he wouldn't be able to cope in school? In life?

Acceptance

He arrived home safely and without incident from school that afternoon, and thus began his school career.

He is about to enter grade four in a few days. While the school is not the ideal setting for him, I'm convinced we made the right choice sending him there. Kids and adults in the community know him and his specialness, and he is greeted in the hallways and welcomed by the school as the special boy that he is. They marvel at his skills, and the school has wisely used his skills to help him teach other children and spark social interaction. His peers at school have learned which behaviours to ignore and which to encourage. I've heard them on the schoolyard playground saying, "C'mon, Nicholas, you can try it!" and reprimanding an older student for yelling because "it hurts Nicholas' ears."

School mates drop by the house to play.

And the past few years we have explored other treatments.

He still sees a homeopath, although we are still waiting for his similimum to be found. We have seen bursts in language and social interaction, but have not seen the kind of progress with the homeopathy we had hoped for.

We tried the much-touted vitamin B6 and magnesium supplements, but the powder was so bitter, no matter what it was mixed with, that he refused to take it.

We removed all dairy and wheat from his diet for a period of three months in the hope of seeing the kind of changes we had read about from autism literature. Nothing. At the end of three months we concluded we had given it a good chance and saw no change in his behaviour, and so went out for ice cream.

Next, DMG (Dimethylglycine). I think he was taking that for six months or so. Again, no change.

I read of a food supplement called Mannatech, and spent a small fortune sending away for that and trying it for four months. There was a combination of supplements that had to be taken together to be effective, but Nicholas refused one of them, try to hide it in food as I may – he could detect it a mile away, so that faltered. We still have about two hundred dollars worth in the pantry.

Brain Gym. I was interested in this program which used simple physical postures and movements to target certain brain centres and prepare these brain centers for certain kinds of activities. It claimed to help children concentrate and learn easier. Nicholas and I went for several private sessions and got a daily program to follow. Non-compliance on Nicholas' part made the program a chore and eventually we dropped it.

A couple of years ago I heard about a computer program that was helpful for children with learning disabilities. It was being promoted primarily for children who had difficulty reading. Its premise was that neural pathways in the brain could be stimulated and awakened by the use of different sounds for children to distinguish, which could then help them to read. Well, Nicholas had no difficulty reading, but he did have difficulty distinguishing which sounds to attend to, so maybe this would be helpful for him, and work in a similar way to auditory training, a treatment we had considered but rejected as the benefits seemed unreliable statistically, and because of Nicholas' non-compliance we envisioned a struggle and a great deal of money down the drain.

But this computer program intrigued us. So we set it up in our home under the guidance of our private speech and language therapist, and we administered the program – two hours a day – over a period of six weeks.

We did see improvement in his focus and attention to other people's conversations as well as his conversation skills.

During this time we also became aware of what we would later learn was synesthesia, the experience of crossed sensory channels. For instance, tasting smells, or hearing colours. Nicholas had always talked of letters of the alphabet and words having colours, but when he started commenting on the colour of the dog's bark, and that he didn't like certain numbers or words because he didn't like their colour, we researched this phenomenon, and are on the lookout for further indications of his synesthesia.

Over the years, his anxiety level has continued to escalate as he gets older, and we have decided to finally come around to trying medication.

The last month of this school year, he was involved in a double blind clinical trial using Ritalin, which did indeed increase his level of focus and attention and decrease what we have come to call his verbal diarrhea, but the after-school rebound factor was a real problem, and most days after school during that last month of grade three he was tantrumming, screaming, and beyond miserable. We took him off it soon after school was out for the year.

And two weeks ago we started him on Paxil at the recommendation of his developmental pediatrician and psychiatrist. We hope that it might serve the same purpose as the Ritalin as far as increasing focus and decreasing the racing of his mind, but without the side-effects. We are also hoping the Paxil will take the edge off his extreme anxiety and obsessive tendencies. So far, we haven't seen any negative side-effects, and last night we noticed he didn't freak out when his favourite show wasn't on – he just turned it to a different station and left the room. Wow!

So, here we are. Five years after his initial diagnosis. We have come to a place of, if not acceptance, a more balanced life. Nicholas still takes center stage, but now I accept work when it comes along, and don't feel guilty at the respite work gives me. We no longer spend every waking moment teaching Nicholas things. We try to have a normal life as much as possible now, every family member's needs being important.

And the five stages? I wish I could believe, now that I've gone through them, that that will be that, and they are behind me. But I suspect I will revisit them time and time again, with each milestone that we encounter. But I will know what to expect the next time around, and maybe they will be a little easier to deal with.

So here we are. The first Monday in September. Labour Day. Speaking of milestones, the day after tomorrow he starts grade four. I'd better get the tissues out.

Grandparents' Day

Knitting

This afternoon as I was in the kitchen preparing dinner, I heard a panicked voice from the study yelling, "I need help!" I dropped the potato peeler and ran. There was Nicholas, in what I have come to recognize as phase one of an autistic tantrum, screaming, "I can't find God's fax number!"

He was seated at the desk with the rolodex open. In the fax machine was a sheet of paper ready to go. I tried to calm him, and asked what he was doing.

"I want to send Oma a fax."

He was getting more anxious.

I pulled the paper out of the machine and turned it over. On it was printed: Dear Oma. What is your mother's sister's middle name? Love Nicholas.

I encouraged him to remain calm and tried to explain, but he had great difficulty accepting the fact that he could fax Grandpa in Vancouver with his obsessive questions about the family tree, but that there was no fax machine in Heaven.

He began pacing the room, very agitated, occasionally flicking his fingers. This was phase two. I quickly had to think of a way to nip this in the bud before he got to phase three, from which there is no easy return.

"I know, why don't we put this in an envelope, and you can take it to Heaven tonight when you go on your plane," I suggested.

Every night when he climbs into bed he insists he is going on his plane, and lists all the places he's going to visit that night. Some nights he's going to go to Dalhousie to give two lectures, then to the grocery store; other nights he's going to Spain and Japan and then to visit his cousins in Ontario. But the itinerary always ends with, "And then I'm going to go to Heaven to have a sleepover with Oma, and then I'll come back here."

So we put the note in an envelope and he prints TO OMA on the front. I suggest that he put it under his pillow so that it will be ready tonight when he goes on his plane. His eyes light up. Phew. One potential explosion averted.

As he runs up to his bedroom, I look over to the framed picture of my mother and smile. He misses his Oma. I miss you too, Mom. Still. A year after you left us. And it hits me at the most unexpected times.

A couple of weeks ago Nic and I were cleaning the basement when I came across my knitting basket. A wave of grief flooded me, my eyes welled up, as I remembered your disheveled knitting basket beside the couch in the rec room, overflowing with skeins of wool, mismatched needles, and dog-eared pattern books. I remembered how I loved days home from school when I was privy to your early afternoon routine: sitting on the couch, knitting, watching your stories. Lulled by the sound of clicking needles, I loved to lie beside you with my toes tucked under your warm doughy thighs.

I remembered the day you taught me to knit; your encouraging words.

I remembered your convincing delight when I presented the canary yellow two-foot by two-foot scarf I made you.

I remembered when I was seventeen how we planned that you would knit my wedding dress.

And I remembered how my heart chilled when, in our last long-distance phone conversation before you died, you complained of being too tired to finish knitting your newest grandchild's christening dress. It was then that I knew you must be very ill indeed, and that soon your knitting needles would be still.

Three weeks later you died.

I don't know how long I sat in the basement, remembering, knitting basket on my lap soaked with tears, but I longed to hear your voice, your laugh; I longed to feel your large Dutch hands rubbing my back the way they used to when I was an upset child. I longed for the "before time," the time before our lives changed forever, the time before we learned of Nicholas' autism.

I miss you.

Through puffy eyes, I took inventory of my knitting basket. I unraveled the half-knit boy's sweater that I had abandoned at the time of Nicholas' diagnosis. I wiped the tears from my eyes and took the basket up to the family room. Into the light. I sat at the end of the couch, opened the pattern, yanked some wool off the skein, cast on, trusted it was like riding a bike, and began knitting.

Nicholas plopped down beside me, and tucked his little feet under my thighs. Genetic instinct I guess. And although he took no interest in what I was doing, when I told him that Oma had knit the afghan he was huddled under, he poked his head out, looked heavenward and yelled, "Thanks for the afghan, Oma!"

And so I'm knitting again. Practically every evening. It has become for me what it must have been for my mother: respite. In her case, from the rigours of raising five children; in my case, from the demands of living with autism. Knitting calms me. It focuses me. It revives me after those particularly frustrating and difficult days with Nicholas: days filled with the relentless and intense pursuit of his obsessions, his aggression and headbanging, days overflowing with frustration all around. Knitting allows me an Autism-Free Zone before bedtime.

Sometimes when I am knitting, I imagine I am knitting Nicholas a thicker skin so that he might find more ease with the world. Some nights I imagine I am knitting back together my frayed nerves. Some nights I even imagine that I am knitting a huge cocoon that will envelop us and keep the world at bay.

But tonight, I will be working on the left armhole in Nicholas' sweater, and I could sure use my mother's expertise. Wish I could just call her up. Or fax. Yes, maybe it's time that God joined the twenty-first century and got a fax machine. It would sure make all our lives a lot easier.

Thanksgiving

Small Miracles

I wanted the Thanksgiving after September 11th to be extra special. A celebration.

My first thought was that we should be with extended family. Maybe we could fly to Vancouver to spend the holiday with David's eighty-two year old father. But Nicholas' panic at the thought of boarding an airplane since the events of September made that choice a non-starter. Shades of *Rainman*.

We considered flying David's father out East to us for the holiday, but after proposing the idea to him, realized the long trip would be too much for him.

So the next best thing was to invite the closest thing to family we have here in Halifax, our friends John and Lita, to enjoy Thanksgiving dinner with us.

I called and invited them. They were delighted to accept.

The planning began two weeks before the big day. I really wanted to create an evening that would make Martha Stewart (revered home-making goddess) proud. No, not proud. Jealous.

I spent hours poring over recipes before coming up with the Thanksgiving dinner menu:

butternut squash soup

cornish hens rotisseried on the barbecue

homemade cranberry sauce

my mother's scalloped potatoes

late carrots from our garden

brussel sprouts with garlic butter

homemade blueberry pie made with wild blueberries from our yard

This menu seemed to me to strike the right note of pioneer chic.

Fittingly, we would eat at the antique pine harvest table in the dining room.

The menu having been decided, I made my shopping lists and created a timetable for all the preparations, working backwards from Thanksgiving day, so I knew what had to be done by when.

First, the house had to get cleaned. Not the best housekeeper in the world (well, I'm neat but not particularly clean), I decided it was time to pay serious homage to the housecleaning gods and really give the house a thorough going-over. Taking into account my over-forty diminished energy level and my after-school responsibilities and the constant interruptions from Nicholas, I calculated this would take me about three days.

Next on the list was decorating. I dismissed the idea of haystacks and groupings of pumpkins and gourds in the corners of the house – I mean, too much pioneer and not enough chic – I decided to focus on a beautifully set table and inviting lighting. Lots of candles.

· I added polishing candlesticks to the 'to do' list.

Shopping. I called ahead to the poultry guy at the farmer's market and pre-ordered the Cornish hens, to be picked up the day before thanksgiving.

I was organized. I was a Thanksgiving dynamo. Martha, move over!

By the day before Thanksgiving, I was on top of things and feeling good: The house was spotless. The pets were given strict instructions not to have any accidents or leave any of their hair anywhere on the premises. In fact, if they preferred to play outside for the entire day, that would be just fine. The shopping was done. The "who does what in the kitchen" list was made and posted so that everyone knew their responsibilities and timelines. The barbecue rotisserie equipment was cleaned and inspected. The propane level in the tank was checked. The blueberries had been picked by Nicholas, David and me the day before. The cranberry sauce was settling nicely in the refrigerator. Firewood for the woodstove had been brought in and stacked beside the hearth.

Thanksgiving morning I awoke before the others, and the first thing on my agenda for that day was to set the table.

I arranged the chairs and added one from the family room to make five.

It was still dark outside. I unfolded my mother's white damask tablecloth (that David had ironed the day before) and smoothed it on the table. I placed two sparkling antique silver candlesticks down the center of the table, and stuck a white candle in each stick. I placed hurricane shades over them.

I opened the buffet cupboard and took out five dinner plates. The fancy white dishes with the rim of silver that rarely got used. I placed them around the table. Atop each plate I placed a matching soup bowl.

I slid the polished silver napkins rings over each napkin and placed them in each bowl. Simple but elegant.

Silver cutlery that my parents gave me on my twenty-fifth birthday was removed from the buffet drawer and set beside each place setting.

The crystal wine glasses that were a wedding gift from my brother were washed and placed to the right of each plate, including Nicholas' place. He could have gingerale mixed with sparkling water for his 'wine' on this special occasion. Water goblets were handwashed and placed beside the wine glasses.

The finishing touch to the table was sitting in a bucket of tepid water in the kitchen. Flowers. I cleaned out a glass flower bowl, and filled it with the cut flowers from the bucket. I arranged and rearranged until it was just right. I carried the vase into the dining room and placed it between the two candlesticks on the table.

I stood for a moment, watching the sunrise over the trees outside, and surveyed the table. I imagined my family and friends sitting around it, the light from the candles playing off the crystal, glass, and dishes. I could smell the flowers and delicious food. I could hear the conversation and laughter.

I sighed. All was good. It was perfect.

By then the boys were getting up and coming downstairs.

After they fed the pets their breakfast, I made Nicholas his usual breakfast of cereal, bacon and apple slices and fruit juice. David took care of himself, and I made myself a couple of pieces of toast with grape jelly.

After breakfast, Nicholas called the local weather office as he does every morning. Today was going to be cool with a twenty percent chance of showers early in the afternoon. That was fine. The showers would be long gone by dinnertime, and the cool temperature meant we could sit around the fire before and after dinner, safe and dry and thankful.

We reviewed the list of who was doing what today. David's jobs were to split the squash; clean, skewer, and barbecue the hens;

lay the fire in the woodstove; and be in charge of cocktails and wine. Nicolas was to pick the carrots from the garden after lunch; help me roll the pie pastry; help load the dishwasher; and tidy up his toys before the guests arrived. He and I also composed a list of possible topics of conversation for when John and Lita were here.

My tasks were everything else.

Our guests were due to arrive at four o'clock. No problem. We were organized and on schedule.

This was going to be the most spectacular Thanksgiving ever.

David showered and dressed. Nic got dressed and washed up. I decided to throw on some sweats and shower after all the prep was done and after my nap that afternoon.

I started with the soup. Once that was made, it could simply be reheated before dinner.

Next was dessert. The pie could be baked and then warmed up in the oven when we sat down to dinner. Nic was very helpful washing the berries and rolling the dough. Very helpful. A little too helpful perhaps. But he enjoyed himself, and I cleaned up the mess when he was done.

Before lunch I had time to season the cleaned birds and return them to the refrigerator.

Rushed light lunch.

I peeled potatoes and assembled them according to my mother's recipe. I covered them and placed them in the now very full refrigerator.

Brussel sprouts were the last thing before nap time. I washed them and peeled away their outer leaves and criss-crossed the stem and put them in a bowl to be steamed later. I set out the garlic and butter for the sauce.

Nap time. Before I went upstairs to lie down, I asked David to lay the fire sooner than later, and told Nic that Dad would take care of whatever he wanted or needed while I had my nap. Nic didn't like me lying down during the day, as it contradicts his rule that 'people sleep at night and not in the day' but I had prepared him for this a couple of days ago, and he was OK with it after I suggested he make a "Do Not Disturb" sign for my bedroom door. Besides, I told him to keep an eye on his watch – I explained that was an expression that meant check the time – because at three o'clock he was to go out to the garden with the bowl I had set by the back door and pick all the carrots that were left in the garden, and then we would cook them and eat them for our special dinner.

I left him with his eyes glued to his watch.

I woke up feeling groggy and just wanting to roll over and sleep more. But I told myself that I would be grateful later. I dozily glanced at the clock and saw that it was three-ten. I had overslept! I had to get moving! Our guests were due in less than an hour!

I never should have had that nap.

I headed to the bathroom to turn on the shower. I looked out the window to the back vegetable garden, expecting to see Nicholas picking carrots for tonight's dinner.

There he was all right, his sweater on backwards, sitting on a rock in the middle of the garden, with an empty bowl on his lap, his face covered with dirt and a half-eaten carrot hanging out of the corner of his mouth like a cigar. Yes, he had picked the carrots, but he had eaten them all!

I ran downstairs and banged out the back door, wondering if I should have written the instructions rather than just verbalizing them, wondering where David was, understanding the temptation of fresh carrots, and angry that he didn't have the sense to wash them first. He calmly greeted me as I approached, unaware that he was doing anything wrong. I dragged him inside and explained why I was upset and cleaned him up, and threw the half of the last carrot into the compost pail.

I shouldn't have taken that nap.

After I'd calmed down I realized that our Thanksgiving feast would still be perfect without carrots.

John and Lita were due in half an hour.

It was then that I heard the first clap of thunder. What? Yes, the weather office had said there was a possibility of showers this afternoon, but no one said anything about a thunderstorm!

Before the rain started to pelt down, David and I managed to dash outside and put the cover on the barbecue. We agreed that the rain would stop by the time the hens had to go on the rotisserie. And even if it was still raining, David could barbecue in his raincoat and ridiculous umbrella hat he won at the county fair last year.

No problem. We could deal with a little thunderstorm. It wasn't going to dampen our plans.

I asked him if the house smelled smoky to him. He sniffed and said no. I went to the woodstove and opened the door. The wood was smoking and I could see it was bubbling at the ends. Damp wood. Great. I closed the door and hoped that the fire would get hot enough to dry the wood and get a good blaze going. I opened a window and tried to fan the smoke outside.

Our guests were due in fifteen minutes.

I had to shower!

Another clap of thunder. The storm was moving closer.

As I hit the bottom of the staircase I heard a retching noise. Similar to the sound the mouth of hell might make when opening up. It came from the basement.

I turned on my heel. Instead of going upstairs, I was going downstairs. The mouth of hell sound again. I turned on my heel again and called up to David to accompany me downstairs. I was about to describe the sound when we both heard it again. From the bowels of the earth this sound came.

David looked at me and whispered that it sounded like it was coming from the rock room. Our house was built around a huge rock in the back of the basement, and when we moved in David and I had joked that the rock was probably the plug in the drain leading to Hell, and we pledged never to attempt to move that rock, or else our house would get sucked down into Hell.

Again the sound. I squeezed David's hand, convinced it was coming from the rock room. I was frightened. And angry that our house was about to get sucked into Satan's inferno on the day of our big dinner party.

Holding on to each other, we crept down the stairs, on the lookout for demons. An otherworldly stench hit our noses. David grabbed a golf club at the bottom of the stairs, like that was going to keep us safe from Satan's clutches, and we felt our way to the light switch. Steeling himself, David flicked on the switch.

Vanna the dog had thrown up all over the basement floor.

Relieved that our house wasn't destined to be dragged into the eternal fires of Hell that day, and that our dinner plans were still a go, I patted David on the shoulder and left him to clean up the mess and tend to the dog.

I headed for the shower.

Then the phone rang. As David was up to his wrists in dog puke, I had no choice but to answer it. It was Lita. They were going to be late as they were having a cat emergency. What was it with pets on Thanksgiving? Their exotic cat Langley had wandered out of their house for the first time in his life and had climbed a tree and was stuck up there. John was in the process of getting a ladder, and as soon as they had Langley down and safe in the house, they would be on their way.

No problem. Gave me more time for my shower.

Another clap of thunder. The storm was directly overhead now.

I looked at the clock and realized it was time to turn on the oven for the scalloped potatoes. I set it for three hundred and fifty degrees and walked to the refrigerator. I could hear Nicholas in the family room trying to engage the cat in a game of Hangman. He was trying to get her to hold a pencil in her paw. The cat was not amused. I pulled the baking dish with the potatoes out of the fridge and inhaled deeply the milky onion bacon potato mixture. I closed the refrigerator door behind me just as a desperate meow and a blur of fur crossed in front of me. In slow motion, I tripped over the cat, the dish slipped from my hands, my mouth fell open and deep slow motion curses came out of my mouth as the dish hit the kitchen floor and shattered – milky onion bacon potato waves crashing slow motion against every visible surface in the kitchen.

Nicholas came running in to the kitchen giggling at the mishap. I ignored his laughter and shooed him out of the kitchen.

Assess the situation. Guests due soon. Not yet showered. No carrots. No scalloped potatoes.

No problem. I would clean up this horrendous mess, ask David to peel more potatoes and chop onion while I was in the shower, and then reassemble and pop the new improved scalloped potatoes into the oven. We just would have to eat a little later than planned. Done.

I walked to the pantry to get the dustpan, the fastest way I thought to begin to scoop up this mess, and David came into the kitchen reeking of puke to ask what had happened. He took one look at the floor and walls and cupboards and turned around and headed back downstairs. I called after him to find the bleeping cat and put her outside. Preferably for the whole winter.

Just then the four o'clock dog started to bark. My back teeth clenched. That high-pitched, annoyingly rhythmic bark that can be heard from some yard in our neighbourhood every single day at exactly the same time. The owners must have it rigged up to a timer or something. I'd like to rig them up to a timer.

As I got on my knees with the dustpan, another loud clap of thunder. The house went black. Power outage. Great.

If I had had a towel in my hand, I would have thrown it in. Instead I threw the dustpan onto the floor, and cold milk with bits of onion and raw bacon splashed onto my face.

Nicholas came running in to the room, frightened and anxious, and wanted assurance from me that the power would come back on in exactly seven minutes. Knowing that any wavering on my part would only serve to increase his anxiety, I assured him the power would be back on in seven minutes, and secretly prayed that it would. But the way this afternoon was going, I feared the worst. I coaxed his watch off his wrist so that he wouldn't "keep an eye on it" and handed him his headphones to ease the noise of the thunder.

If only I hadn't taken that stupid nap.

Vanna the dog started to bark. Badly out of rhythm with the four o'clock dog. I closed my eyes and took four long breaths through my nose.

David stumbled upstairs in the dark, and lit the candles from my beautiful dining room table, and brought them into the kitchen. Between claps of thunder and having to reassure our pacing, flapping, and refusing-to-be-held-or-comforted son that everything would be back to normal in a few minutes, David and I sat in the candlelit kitchen and reconnoitered.

No power meant no water from our well, so no shower. For either Ms. Scalloped Potato Face or Mr. Dog Puke Shirt.

Backup plan. Who would have thought we'd need a backup plan?

We could remake the scalloped potatoes. When the power returned we could pop those in the oven. We had no carrots but we still could have steamed brussel sprouts when the power returned. And we still had soup. In fact, we could probably serve the soup cold. Very shi-shi. And the barbecue didn't require electricity so cooking the hens wasn't a problem. And of course we had the pie. No problem.

David started peeling by the light of the candles. I went to the family room to check on Nic's anxiety level and stoke up the fire.

Nicholas was lying on the couch with his flashlight, upset because his favourite game show was due to come on and he was going to miss the beginning of it because the power was out and "I hate it when the power goes out and my emotions are sick and I have a headache." I sat with him and tried to calm him. I suggested that he get his sleeping bag – his cocoon as he calls it – and get a book and pretend to camp out in the family room and get in his sleeping bag and read a book by the flashlight. Thankfully, he was keen and David interrupted his potato peeling to guide Nicholas up to his room to fetch his camping supplies.

I went to the woodstove and opened the door. Damp yellow smoke hit my face. The fire was out. That darn damp wood. And that darn nap!

I grabbed a couple of pieces of firewood from the hearth. Damp as well. And the wood outside was soaked from the storm.

So no fire.

Nicholas zipped himself into his sleeping bag in the middle of the floor.

David yelped from the kitchen. He nicked himself with the potato peeler.

I told him the bad news about the fire. Dashed was the hope that we could cook veggies on top of the woodstove if the power stayed off.

We would have to barbecue the vegetables.

Corn, zucchini, pepper slices, sure, but how did one barbeque brussel sprouts and scalloped potatoes?

I instructed David to stop his peeling. We would have baked potatoes on the barbecue with the Cornish hens and I would somehow rig up little foil packets of sprouts in garlic butter.

No problem.

Another clap of thunder. It sounded like the storm was hovering right over our house and showed no signs of moving on.

I smiled weakly at David and took a candle to the front closet and fetched his raincoat, boots, and umbrella hat. I assured him that no matter how goofy he looked – and he did look pretty goofy – no neighbours would see him as it was getting dark outside and all the streetlamps were off. I handed him a flashlight and pushed him out the back door and into the stormy dusk.

I was on my knees cleaning up the scalloped potato mess by candlelight when he came inside and shook himself off. Nicholas was still cozy in his sleeping bag, reading out loud.

Ten minutes later the goo was mopped up and the barbecue was heated. I handed David the birds and together we skewered them and attached the rotisserie motor to the skewer. We both clued in at the same moment: the rotisserie motor required electricity to turn the spit!

As tears welled up in my scalloped-potato-encrusted eyes, David put his arm around me. As I blubbered about the beautiful dinner I had planned and what a disaster this day was turning out to be, he opened a bottle of wine and poured me a big glass. I took a long drink and dried my eyes. I felt like I was in a bad TV sitcom.

He checked his watch. Five-fifteen. He took charge as it was clear I was no longer capable.

First he would call John and Lita and check on their situation and attempt to get an idea as to when they expected to arrive. He dug the cell phone out of my purse. Dead battery.

As we had no way to make contact with them, David decided that we would eat when the food was ready, and they would arrive when they arrived.

As for the revised menu, David suggested we cut up the hens and barbecue them flat on the grill. And we'd still have the foil packet sprouts, and we could put the pie on the barbecue to reheat.

No problem.

We cut up the hens in the dim light, careful not to chop ends off fingers.

A glass of wine later, they were ready to go on the barbecue. David resumed his rain costume and headed back out. I cupped my hands around my eyes and pressed my nose against the back door and watched him lift the barbecue lid and put the meat on the grill. I could hear Nicholas reading another book.

I made foil packets into which I placed five brussel sprouts and a dab of butter and minced garlic. I folded them up carefully and put them on a platter for David to pick up on his next kitchen pit stop.

I put grapes and crackers on a plate and took it into Nicholas for a camping snack, as dinner was going to be late.

It was then that I heard the scream.

I ran out the back door to the sight of high flames rising up from the barbecue. As David turned toward me, I noticed smoke wafting off his chin. His beard had been singed! Without saying anything I ran back into the kitchen and grabbed wads of paper towel and turned on the tap to soak them. Nothing. No water. We'd used up all our reserve tank in cleaning up. I ran back outside and pointed to the garden. I was jumping up and down but no words were coming out of my mouth. I ran to him, pointing and trying to sputter words. I grabbed his hand and pulled him to the garden and dunked his face into the bird bath.

He raced back to the barbecue and turned it off. The flames immediately died down leaving the shriveled bits of blacked hen sizzling as the pouring rain doused the smoke.

This time it was my turn to be strong. I left the lid of the barbecue up to let the rain extinguish any lingering smoke, and abandoned the whole mess, and led David back to the kitchen. I took off his coat and boots, and hat, and held a candle close to his face, but not too close, to assess the damage to his beautiful beard. I concluded that a closer than usual trim at the barber would take care of it, and handed him a candle to go survey the ruins in the hall mirror.

Oblivious Nicholas was on to his third book.

OK. No hens. No sprouts. No potatoes. I poured another glass of wine and revised the menu once again.

I asked David the time. Six-thirty. Even though John and Lita had not yet arrived, I decided it was time for dinner.

I returned the candles to the center of the table. I called David and Nicholas into the dining room. Nicholas complained that he wanted to finish his book first. I wasn't going to argue. Not today.

Another clap of thunder.

David and I took our seats, waiting for our son to finish his book. We sat, listening to him read. As I turned to call to Nicholas, there was a crack, my chair broke, and I was on the floor. David leaned over to help me up, asking if I was all right. Our eyes met in a straw-that-broke-the-camel's-back kind of moment.

I forget which of us started laughing first. I think we've been married long enough that it was simultaneous.

Another clap of thunder.

Nicholas came into the dining room where I was on my back laughing hysterically and David was laughing helplessly on his knees beside me.

Nicholas asked if we had said anything he didn't like. Getting no response but guffaws, he asked if someone had told a joke.

I giggled, "Yeah, why do elephants have wrinkly skin? Because they hate to iron."

David and I roared, while Nicholas objected because elephants don't iron.

I gulped air and bellowed, "Why did Tigger have his head in the toilet? He was looking for Pooh!!"

Another roar from the hysterical parents. Another correction from the autistic child. "You mean Winnie the Pooh, Jennifer," he protested.

As Nicholas took his seat at the dining room table, he said, "Mom and Dad are having a wacky day."

Another roar. I was afraid I would wet my pants.

When the giggles subsided, David helped me up and he brought around one of the vacant chairs for me to sit in.

I looked at the table. It was beautiful. So were the faces around it.

David, my husband of twelve years, more handsome than ever despite his singed beard and pukey shirt.

My special son, his blue eyes serious and innocent.

And me, unshowered, and caked with raw scalloped potatoes, feeling really happy.

David poured more wine for us, and gingerale for Nicholas.

I began to serve the cold squash soup with a dollop of cranberry sauce, and the cold blueberry pie.

David suggested that we might want to make a toast as it was Thanksgiving. He raised his glass, and in his deep, resonant voice said, "I'm thankful that we are together and happy."

We sipped. We told Nicholas to sip his gingerale.

I raised my glass, and told my boys, "I'm very thankful for having you both in my life."

We sipped. Nic sipped his gingerale.

David asked Nicholas if he would like to make a toast. Nicholas thought that meant sipping his gingerale. But before the glass reached his lips, David returned it to the table, and explained to Nicholas what a toast is and what being thankful means. He asked Nicholas to name something he was thankful for.

Without hesitation Nicholas said, "I'm thankful for the alphabet."

We all sipped.

Another clap of thunder.

A knock on the front door. John and Lita had arrived.

As Nicholas skipped down the hall to answer the front door, I looked across the table to David and said, "Something else to be thankful for."

"Absolutely", he replied.

We clinked glasses.

October 22nd: Nicholas' Birthday

The Conversation

J: Nic, are you finished with your breakfast?

N: Yes, I'm done. I don't want the rest of my Cheerios.

J: OK, take your pills, and then I want us to have a conversation in the family room.

N: What about?

J: Well um, about you.

N: Yeah. I'll take my pills.

J: OK. I'll sit here. Where do you want to sit?

N: Here on this green spot. This green cushion.

J: OK. How old are you?

N: I'm the big nine. I'm going to put my head behind you. Lean back. Tighter. Tighter.

     (*Nicholas sits up*)

J: OK, now can we talk?

N: Yes.

J: So, I want to talk to you about...

N: About what?

J: Well, about you.

N: OK. That's fine.

J: OK? Now, you know that we sometimes go to see Dr. Hawkins.

N: OK.

J: Yeah. Why do you think we do that?

N: I'm not sure.

J: Do you think... Do you know other kids that go to see Dr. Hawkins?

N: I think we're the only people.

J: Yeah?

N: Because since I don't see other kids at Dr. Hawkins or maybe they do but I don't see them do it? (*sneeze*)

J: Gesundheit! Maybe you're allergic to being nine years old!

N: No, that's silly. (*sneeze*)

J: Gesundheit again! You are Mr. Sneezy this morning. So you think that maybe other kids go to see Dr. Hawkins but we just don't see them there?

N: (*nods*)

J: Yeah? Maybe. So, what kind of doctor is Dr. Hawkins?

N: A regular doctor. Or is she a normal doctor?

J: Well...

N: It means the same thing.

J: Yeah. She's a... she's a doctor for special kids. Ummm, what about...let's talk about school for a minute. What about school? What about Ms. Williams? Does she help just you in the classroom, or all the kids in the classroom?

N: I believe all the kids.

J: Yes, that's true, but she mostly helps you, doesn't she? She sits beside you in the classroom doesn't she?

N: 'Cause that's the most time she has.

J: And what kind of things does she do for you? What are the things she helps you with?

N: Spelling and math.

J: Yeah? I thought you were great at spelling and math. Maybe there are some other things she helps you with.

N: (*nods*)

J: Like what?

N: Ummm, I'm not sure.

J: Like what about when Ms. Ferguson reads a story to the class. Do you have trouble listening to that?

N: Yes.

J: Yeah.

N: Do you think it's because I don't think hard?

J: Well, no...I think, I think that...

N: Is it a tough one?

J: Yeah, it's tough for you. To listen to things, isn't it?

N: (*nods*)

J: Because...

N: Because I have my earphones on because I have sensitive ears?

J: You have sensitive ears – that's exactly right.

N: That's true.

J: Now, do you think all the kids in your class have sensitive ears or just you?

N: No, I think I'm the only one.

J: You're the only one. So, there's a reason why you have sensitive ears. And there's a reason why you don't like to be touched.

N: 'Cause they can knock me.

J: Yeah, and you don't like that do you?

N: 'Cause that hurts.

J: Yeah. And what about when I just touch you like that – does that hurt?

N: No.

J: No. Well. Ms. Williams is in the classroom to help you with some things you have difficulty with, and we go and see Dr. Hawkins, and sometimes Dr. Orlik.

N: Yeah.

J: Because...you are a very special boy. Remember how we talked about how your brain is a little bit different from other people's brains? Remember we talked about that because you sometimes get frustrated when I don't remember things as well as you do, right? And I told you that what is in my brain might be different from what is in your brain, right?

N: Right.

J: You have an excellent memory. You remember everything, don't you? Not everyone can remember things as well as you can. What other things are you good at?

N: I'm not sure.

J: You're great at spelling. You've always been great at spelling.

N: I'm great at math.

J: And yes, you're great at math.

N: Am I great at language arts?

J: Yes.

N: And was I great at copying my homework from the board?

J: Yes, you still are.

N: Yeah!

J: But I want to tell you why you're so great at some things and you have some difficulty with some other things.

N: Like...how about autumn shoes and spring shoes? I have difficulty with them.

J: You have difficulty with that?

N: Tying them up.

J: Oh yes, that's true. And you have some difficulty with riding your bike.

N: Yeah.

J: Yeah. That's why we have to practise that. So, you think maybe you're a little bit different from some of the other kids at school?

N: (*long pause*) Yeah.

J: Because your brain works a little bit differently from the other kids'. It's a great brain. You have a very special brain. But you have…ummm…and your friend Tommy has...autism. (*pause*) Have you heard that word before?

N: How do you spell that?

J: A-U-T-I-S-M

N: What does it mean?

J: Well, it means…it's a word that describes…

N: A place, a balcony.

J: No, it's a word that describes how your brain is different from my brain and Dad's brain and the brains of the kids at school. It describes what makes you special. You have autism.

N: Yeah.

J: And it means that you're really smart at some things, but you have some difficulty with other things.

N: Yeah.

J: And that's why Ms. Williams is there to help you at school –

       (*Nicholas gets up and starts to leave the room*)

J: Nic, we're not done yet buddy. Why are you leaving?

N: Because I feel like it.

J: Well, we're not finished our conversation yet. Come back and sit on the couch beside me.

N: No. I want to stay here.

J: You won't be able to hear me from there.

N: Yes I will.

J: Well, I'm worried I won't be able to hear you from here.

N: Yes you can. I'll talk louder.

J: OK.

N: I'll pretend that I'm standing on the blue spot right there.

J: OK. So. Autism. Uh, so that's why Dad and I help you practise certain things –

N: Are we finished?

J: No, and that's why we're so proud of you –

N: You mean embarrassed! Be embarrassed!

J: – sorry, embarrassed, that you're doing so great at swimming –

N: (*getting anxious*) Are we done now? How many minutes – how many more things do we have to say?

J: About seven.

N: Yes. Can we do ten or is that too much? Can we do ten or is that too much!!!

J: That's fine. We can do ten if you like. So…

N: Let's do three more.

J: Yeah, that's fine. So. Autism.

    (*Nicholas cringes*)

J: Are you frustrated?

N: Yes, I've had enough.

J: Have you? Is it upsetting you that we're talking about this?

N: Yes, I really want to go play Super Mario.

J: Well, in three minutes you can go play Super Mario, OK?

N: Two minutes now! Two minutes please! OK, two minutes! Say two minutes!!!

J: OK.

N: Or four minutes! Can I have four minutes?!!!

J: Yes.

N: Whatever, my choice?

J: Whatever, your choice. What's your choice?

N: Zero minutes.

       (*Jennifer shakes her head*)

N: OK, I hope the conversation's not for long!

J: No, it won't be long.

N: Not for long!!!! Not for long!!!!

J: Can I just explain a little bit more about autism?

N: Yes.

J: OK. Autism means… Having autism or being autistic means that you have difficulty learning how to have proper conversations, yes?

N: Yes.

J: And that you have very sensitive ears.

N: Yes.

J: And it means that you don't like to be touched.

N: Right.

J: Right? You don't like to be hugged, or kissed.

N: Right.

J: And it also means that you're very smart, and that...ummmmm, sometimes you need to learn about proper behaviour.

N: What does that mean?

J: Well –

N: Time outs?

J: Yeah, well, it means that we use time outs to teach you how to behave and learn what is good behaviour and what is bad behaviour. So that you can learn how to behave properly. What is appropriate behaviour and what is not appropriate behaviour. And you need to learn how to have great conversations and play with friends. Yes?

(Nicholas nods his head)

J: So, if somebody asks you, "Nicholas why don't you like to be touched?" What could you say?

N: I don't know!!

J: Well, you could say, "Because I have autism."

N: Mom, can I go play Super Mario downstairs?! I really need to! Now I'm done!

J: OK, buddy. Our conversation's done. Do you want to get dressed first?

N: No! Or do I have to?

J: No, you can get dressed after you play Super Mario.

N: I'm not going to play Super Mario!

J: Oh. All right.

N: Mom, is Dad going to be in the bathroom for a short time or a long time? Which do you think? What does he usually tend to do?

J: We'll have to wait and see. He tends to be in the bathroom for a short time.

N: What about yesterday?

J: Oh, was he in there for a long time yesterday?

N: Do you think so?

J: Yeah, I guess so.

N: How come? 'Cause it was what?

J: I think it's private what goes on in the bathroom, so I didn't ask.

N: Because it was his birthday, is that why?

J: Yes, that must be why.

N: Do you think he had a relaxing time in there?

J: Yes, I'm sure he did.

N: Yeah. See ya. I'm going downstairs.

J: OK, sweetie. Love you.

      (*pause*)

J: What do you say?

N: Love you too.

J: And remember, Nicholas, you are special. And if you have any questions about autism or being autistic, you come and ask me or Dad. OK?

N: See ya.

(*Nicholas goes downstairs*)

J: (*whispering*) Or maybe Dad and I should ask you questions about autism and being autistic.

Postscript

A Letter to My Son

Dear Nicholas,

I'm so sorry you were upset about our conversation yesterday. Although you couldn't tell me exactly what was bothering you, I know that you didn't want to talk about autism, did you? That's why you wanted to leave the room and go play, isn't it?

I'm sorry. I wasn't very good at talking about it either. I never meant to upset you.

Now that you are nine years old, you are old enough to start understanding yourself, and your specialness. You are our big boy now.

Remember what I said. It's not a bad thing to have autism. It's just a word to describe how your brain is a little different from ours. And the kids' at school.

Different. You are different. And that is such a great thing to be. When you are a little older, we'll talk about and read about some very different people in history who did some awesome things. All because their brains were a little different from everyone else's.

Your brain is very special. Dad and I hope you will learn to love it. That means like it a lot because of all the great things it can do.

So don't ever think that because you are different you are bad or dumb.

Unique. That's it. That's a fun word. It's French, but we use it in English now too.

You are unique.

So, when you are calmer about it, and have had some time to think about autism, Dad and I hope that the three of us can sit down and talk about it some more. Would that be OK? No rush. Whenever you are ready. Whenever you are ready to hear. Whenever you are ready to talk. We'll be here.

We'll always be here for you.

Dad and I are so proud of you. You've taken many giant steps in the past five years.

And on the long road that stretches out before you, I know that you will touch many lives and hearts. You captured ours long ago.

And maybe somewhere along that road we can all sit down together and rest and look at this book of snapshots and laugh and remember.

Whenever you're ready, son, we'll be there…

Love Mom